Gender Violence in the American Southwest (AD 1100–1300)

This volume uses osteobiography and individual-level analyses of burials retrieved from the La Plata River Valley (New Mexico) to illustrate the variety of roles that Ancestral Pueblo women played in the past (circa AD 1100–1300). The experiences of women as a result of their gender, age, and status over the life course are reconstructed, with consideration given to the gendered forms of violence they were subject to and the consequences of social violence on health. The authors demonstrate the utility of a modern bioarchaeological approach that combines social theories about gender and violence with burial data in conjunction with information from many other sources—including archaeological reconstruction of homes and communities, ethnohistoric resources available on Pueblo society, and Pueblo women's contemporary voices. This analysis presents a more accurate, nuanced, and complex picture of life in the past for mothers, sisters, wives, and, captives.

Debra L. Martin is a Distinguished Professor of Anthropology at the University of Nevada, Las Vegas NV, USA.

Claira E. Ralston is a PhD Candidate in the Department of Anthropology at the University of Nevada, Las Vegas NV, USA.

T0347443

Bodies and Lives
Series Editor: Anna Osterholtz

Gender Violence in the American Southwest (AD 1100–1300)
Mothers, Sisters, Wives, Slaves

**Debra L. Martin and
Claira E. Ralston**

Routledge
Taylor & Francis Group

LONDON AND NEW YORK

First published 2023
by Routledge
4 Park Square, Milton Park, Abingdon, Oxon OX14 4RN

and by Routledge
605 Third Avenue, New York, NY 10158

Routledge is an imprint of the Taylor & Francis Group, an informa business

British Library Cataloguing-in-Publication Data
A catalogue record for this book is available from the British Library

ISBN: 978-0-367-64223-5 (hbk)
ISBN: 978-0-367-64227-3 (pbk)
ISBN: 978-1-003-12352-1 (ebk)

DOI: 10.4324/9781003123521

Typeset in Times New Roman
by MPS Limited, Dehradun

This volume is dedicated to all the women in the world who suffer at the hands of others.

Contents

Figures

Table

Acknowledgments

We would like to thank Anna Osterholtz (Series Editor) for her help in bringing this work to fruition and Katherine Ong (Editor at Routledge) for her guidance and help during the process. We are grateful to our colleagues who read parts of the book and provided helpful feedback, including Pamela K. Stone, Sabrina Agarwal, Pamela Geller, Kathryn Baustian, and Ryan Harrod, and as always to our families and friends. This work was partially funded by the Wenner-Gren Foundation for Anthropological Research #7626.

1 Mindful Bodies

Introduction

Bioarchaeology is a branch of anthropology that focuses on the ethical study of human bodies retrieved from archaeological excavation sites (Martin et al., 2013). It integrates what can be discovered from these ancient burials within a richly configured cultural and historical context using a range of archaeological, forensic, medical, and anthropological techniques. At the center of a bioarchaeological project is the scientific study of human remains using the archaeological record to enhance what can be known about the past. Bioarchaeology helps explain human lifeways and behaviors and it helps explain how and why patterns emerge in cultures at specific points in time. It also provides time depth and a cross-cultural perspective on humans as both biological and cultural beings. This merging of biological and cultural aspects of the lived human experience is referred to as the biocultural approach, which we discuss below.

There are several ethical challenges bioarchaeology currently faces. Bioarchaeology carries the burden of having been largely an activity that was solely carried out by European-American (White) researchers with little or no input from living Indigenous people who were and still are connected culturally and/or biologically with the burials being studied. Pushback and demands for reparations and repatriation of human remains to their living decedents began in the 1980s and continues today (Thomas & Krupa, 2021). Archaeological sites themselves are the creation of early European-American archaeologists' revisionist history agendas, and the monopoly on the practice of locating, naming, excavating, curating, and explaining archaeological materials persists today as part of a colonial mindset, i.e. "I found it, it's mine" (Trabert, 2022). The popular media often take bioarchaeological studies and sensationalize or romanticize the findings in

DOI: 10.4324/9781003123521-1

ways that are often "inappropriate, unethical, and unprofessional" (Squires et al., 2022: 1 citing Passalacqua et al., 2014). Therefore, performing ethical, professional, and appropriate studies using the bodies of individuals who lived a long time ago is fraught with ethical dilemmas and challenges.

These and other challenges and criticisms regarding bioarchaeological research are valid, important, timely, and are part of a larger movement to decolonize archaeology and revitalize how research using archaeological remains is conducted. Readers are encouraged here to look at the chapter by Marek-Martinez (2021) titled "Indigenous Archaeological Approaches and the Refusal of Colonialism in Archaeology" in Panich and Gonzales' (2021) edited volume, *The Routledge Handbook of the Archaeology of Indigenous-Colonial Interaction in the Americas.*

Bioarchaeologists have acknowledged the need to focus on how to create a new future for archaeological-based studies of individuals to whom they are not related. There are many ideas out there about very specific ways to decolonize bioarchaeology, and these are the voices that we have been listening to as we conducted this study. In the SAA Archaeological Record (March 2022, Volume 22, Number 2), Wilcox et al. present an overview of findings based on two listening sessions led by the SAA Task Force on Decolonization (TFD). Decolonization is a trendy term being used as part of a larger move to address both historical inequities in the discipline and the lack of diversity in journals and organizations. The TFD formulated six ideas for decolonizing archaeology (Wilcox et al. 2022: 13). These include (1) being aware and acknowledging the embedded colonial practices within archaeology, such as the destruction of sacred sites, the failure to connect contemporary descendants with their ancestral sites, and the use of language that stereotypes Indigenous people; (2) reconsidering the primary emphasis of archaeology as one of "stewardship" to something else; (3) normalizing collaboration, consultation, and acknowledgments as part of archaeological training and practice; (4) carrying out archaeological projects that include community participation; (5) formulating best practices regarding the impact of research on Indigenous people today; and (6) articulating decolonization practices in North America with those being carried out in Latin America and the Caribbean.

Many Indigenous scholars provide compelling examples of how to make the science of archaeology and bioarchaeology be less exclusive and less reliant on "scientific objectivity." These writers call for the inclusion of Indigenous voices, resources, expert opinions, and community-supported approaches to archaeology. As Marek-Martinez (2021: 503) states,

> Western research has relied on the mechanisms of colonialism to support, uphold, and justify notions about Indigenous peoples and their pasts that result in the displacement of Indigenous voices and perspectives in the past. This has perpetuated harmful ideologies that continue to pervade the research and investigation of and about Indigenous peoples in archaeological research.

The principals of decolonization are not impossible to recognize and incorporate into anthropology, and they produce an archaeological/ bioarchaeological practice that is scientifically sound and respectful, and inclusive of multiple voices in interpreting and narrating the past.

In this work, we focus on questions about gender violence, specifically violence against women, and the ways that this cultural practice burdens targeted women with particularly harmful health effects. Violence and fear of violence profoundly shaped their world views and lived experiences. Gender violence is an ancient human practice that likely endures far back into human history (Martin & Harrod, 2020). We look beyond the archaeological focus on ancient man-on-man violence, men dying in war, warrior men, and raiding by men to focus on the variety of ways that females and women were engaged with or were targets of violence. In Indigenous cultures in ancient North America (AD 800–1400s), there is evidence that women were targeted and victimized as malevolent forces and sorcerers, as captives and enslaved laborers, and as noncombatants and refugees (Cameron, 2016). The bones of these women reveal a partial truth about those cultural practices and how it affected them. This work could not be done without examining the bodies (in this case, the skeletonized remains of the body).

Presenting and Studying Bodies

The bodies of people living in small-scale societies prior to industrialization provide a barometer for how well groups were faring and reflect the adaptive behaviors and coping mechanisms they used to survive. The notion of "the mindful body" comes from Nancy Scheper-Hughes and Margaret Lock (1987) and their expansive examination into how medical anthropologists can best study health care and diseases, particularly in non-Western cultures. Because medical anthropologists are largely trained in the biomedical sciences with its Cartesian approach to focusing solely on the body to the exclusion of the mind, the authors argue that researchers must reimagine what health and disease is like in non-Western groups using different calibrations for how people experienced their bodies and their diseases (Scheper-Hughes & Lock, 1987). They suggest that it is necessary to reframe our point of reference away from Cartesian dualism that separates the mind (internal) from the body (external). Instead, there are plenty of cross-cultural examples where groups do not make this distinction and operate on the assumption that the body itself is "mindful," with no separation in any measurable sense from the body. Mindful bodies interact with and are shaped by a range of cultural, biological, and environmental forces filtered through culturally specific ideologies and ways of understanding. Bioarchaeologists who look at health care and diseases in the deep past benefit from these observations about the mindful body, which invites a more emic approach to past bodies. Emic in this sense means understanding disease and trauma from the point of view of the individuals in their unique moments in time and space versus overlaying existing external frameworks.

Small-scale societies, especially those prior to European colonization, offer an opportunity to understand the origins and evolution of sexual divisions of labor, gendered patterns in exposure to risk, differential life experiences, and the social construction of gender identities. By small-scale societies, we refer to precolonial Indigenous cultural groups that are smaller in size and less politically centralized than large agricultural or city-state societies. Because humans lived exclusively in small-scale societies for well over 100,000 years, they represent a baseline from which to better understand the unfolding and expression of gender in historic and contemporary times.

Archaeologists often use the material culture produced by past people, including stone tools, spear points, ceramics, petroglyphs, iconography, botanical remains, and animal bones to reconstruct how people lived, whereas bioarchaeologists often use burials and the human remains within them to reconstruct how people lived and died. Archaeological reconstructions often focused almost exclusively on men's activities. Traditionally, women's labor and daily activities were not presented in the same ways as men's, and women tended to be superficially described using stereotypic Western paradigmatic portrayals. From archeological studies to museum dioramas, males/men are depicted as engaging in a range of subsistence and economic activities while females/women are relegated to preparing meals and watching over children (Figures 1.1 and 1.2).

As Lonetree (2012) emphasized, many of these dioramas present the colonial viewpoint and narrative of Native Americans as essentially

Figure 1.1 Diorama of a group of Cheyenne along Coal Creek, CO circa 1860. The complete diorama is housed at the North American Indian cultures exhibit in the Denver Museum of Nature and Science. These older dioramas reflect a particular narrative about pre-colonial life that is problematic. Credit: Avrand6, CC BY-SA 4.0. https://creativecommons.org/licenses/by-sa/4.0, via Wikimedia Commons. https://commons.wikimedia.org/wiki/File:Cheyenne_Diorama,_1860s,_Denver_Museum_of_Nature_and_Science.jpg.

timeless relics, static and unchanging, adhering to a rigid division of labor. Not only are these scenarios likely wrong, but they dehumanize past people and relegate them to a past that is unconnected to the present. This reifies a particular narrative about Indigenous peoples as extinct or vanished, when in fact they are living throughout the Americas today and consistently demonstrate deep ancestral connections to many archaeological sites. It is highly unlikely that these static portrayals are realistic given what we know from ethnographic accounts and archaeological reconstructions of small-scale societies, which display a great deal of nuance, change over time, and variability in the contributions of females/women in political, economic, and religious capacities and male's/men's contributions to food processing and childcare. Acknowledging and including the complexity of women's lives in small-scale societies is crucial for reconstructing more

Figure 1.2 Diorama of a Chumash woman and her baby. Women are portrayed in childrearing and food processing domains, while men and young boys appear to be engaged in fishing and building huts. Diorama housed at the Santa Barbara Museum of Natural History. Rigid gender roles are presented as women deal with food and children, and men deal with hunting, fishing, and socializing young boys. Credit: Jllm06, CC-BY-SA-3.0, https://creativecommons.org/licenses/by-sa/3.0/, via Wikimedia Commons. https://commons.wikimedia.org/wiki/File:Santa_Barbara_Museum_of_Natural_History_-_Chumash_diorama.JPG

realistic and less essentialized versions of the history and trajectory of women's dynamic, variable, and influential roles in society.

Furthermore, these dioramas rarely engage with colonialism's hand in genocide, ethnocide, and white supremacy (Sicola, 2020). Hart (2019) provides an overview of recent attempts to decolonize portrayals of Indigenous communities prior to and during colonialization. She shows that even depictions in museums and heritage centers that are based on collaborations that include Indigenous viewpoints are strapped by a colonial legacies and narratives that infiltrate most attempts. As she states, the widespread embeddedness of manifest destiny in American culture relies on notions of colonial progress and vanquished and disappearing Indians. Even in more dynamic presentations of Indigenous gender roles, there is a sense of discontinuity with present-day descendant Indigenous groups, as if these past people have no relationship to those living today.

The vestiges of the bodies of people who died long ago reveal complex (although admittedly partial) truths about human experience and human suffering. Bioarchaeologists, who are trained to read and interpret the preserved skeletal and dental remains of past bodies, can provide a wide range of information on how individuals lived and died (for examples, see Martin & Anderson, 2014). We are particularly interested in violence and trauma, and bodies can reveal a great deal about these conditions. Bioarchaeological studies have the potential to situate modern-day problems within a larger temporal and spatial framework. Using cross-cultural and deep time perspectives, trauma on the body can be understood within a broader temporal framework that can provide a snapshot of when gender violence started in human groups and the nature of its genesis. To operationalize this approach, we provide a case study that focuses on women's roles in a pre-colonial Indigenous group located in what is now modern-day New Mexico in the Southwest United States.

The global call for action in the past year, ranging from the #metoo movement to women's rights marches and protests, reminds us that women are often in positions of being subordinate to forms of structural violence that are kept in place by various forms of patriarchy; or, more explicitly, women are subordinate under a system where men assume leadership positions and keep laws and customs in place that suppress women from operating from positions of power. Violence directed at women by men is often underreported and overlooked because the systemic and institutionalized abuse of females/women is rarely considered an outrage or aberrant in many societies. Instead, it is often considered to be the status quo. Paraphrasing from sociologist Johan Galtung, who has written extensively about the ways that structural violence works, if one man beats one woman, it is seen as a social transgression and engenders outrage, but if one thousand men beat one thousand women, it is met with a shrug of the shoulders and complacency because it has become part of the everyday normal (1969: 171). There are those who think that modern society invented patriarchy, but forms of patriarchy are found also in very early small-scale societies (Martin & Harrod, 2015).

Counterintuitively, the ubiquity and everydayness of violence against women is what renders it invisible, and that is the power of structural violence—subordination, abuse, and marginalization which is tacitly and implicitly sanctioned by those in power. These embedded notions are what normalize violence against women. Because little is done to curb it on a grand scale, it is seen today in antiquated and ambiguously worded laws, policies, and legislation that often make it difficult for women to seek out or obtain justice for their lived experiences of violence and abuse. Much of this abuse is related to the cultural objectification and commodification of women, which raises the question: how far back do these practices go? Is this a function of modernity or does violence against women have a longer history? These are the questions that drive our research and so we look to the archaeological record for answers.

Why a Book on Gender Violence in the Past?

There are publications in the thousands of studies reporting and analyzing patterns of violence against women, and the numbers consistently remain high. The national statistics on intimate nonlethal partner violence is estimated to be 20 individuals every minute, adding up to 10 million women in the United States alone (https://ncadv.org/STATISTICS). One in five women (and one in seventy-one men) on average are raped in their lifetime. Over 30,000 women die each year due to male-initiated violence. Unfortunately, these statistics do not include a wide range of other acts of gender violence, including but not limited to, sexual harassment in the workplace, sexual abuse of children, enslavement and indentured servitude, stalking, and homicide.

Given the difficulty of accurately reporting, documenting, studying, exposing, and diminishing violence that specifically targets women today, revealing gender violence and violence against women in the past is especially important for locating the historical roots and antecedents of gender violence. Anthropologists place violence in a broad environmental, social, and ideological context that considers not just violent encounters, but also cultural beliefs and social structures from which notions about and perceptions of women and women's bodies are embedded. Using an integrative biocultural model, we can look beyond the proximate causes of violence and identify how gender violence becomes embedded within societies, and how this affects women's lives and their bodies. Using a mix of ethnographic, archival, archaeological, and biological approaches, gender violence in the past shines a light on its antiquity and embeddedness in social institutions. More importantly, this kind of study offers ways of thinking holistically about the problem and examining the ultimate causes, not just the proximate ones.

To be clear, humans invented violence against women. There is nothing natural, genetic, or biological about men using violence on women. Some men may be more predisposed toward violence, but the expression of it is primarily related to cultural conditioning and socialization (Tummala-Narra et al., 2020). Gender violence is not random, rather it is intentional, targeted, and focused in ways that almost make it a ritualized behavior. Case after case of gender violence reveals culturally specific ways that women are commodified, objectified, and dehumanized. Particularly for Indigenous women in North America today, their abduction, violent abuse, and murder are rampant in part due to the legacy of colonialism which has marginalized them to the point where blaming the victim is often the fallback response (Hargreaves, 2017). Structural violence plays a role as well. Today, rules, laws, and policies often work against the protection of all women, but especially Indigenous women.

Has violence against women increased or decreased over time? Is violence against women found in every culture? Does it occur in similar ways across different cultures? These are questions for which we have no answers yet. Violence is better understood in the more historical and recent complex societies like Egypt, Rome, and other groups throughout much of Europe. These large, stratified societies have forms of written records in addition to a great deal of archaeological evidence on practices such as warfare, raiding, slavery, and other forms of violence. However, North American archaeologists have focused almost exclusively on the role of men in warfare, weaponry, and defensive architecture. Furthermore, ethnographic and ethnohistoric resources on small-scale societies in the Americas have focused in general more on warfare and/or on the later colonization and genocide of Indigenous groups. The questions we are more interested in are the presence and role of gendered violence in small-scale societies for which there are no written records and for time periods where the archaeological record is all that is available. In this case, we are examining a time period predating the late 1400s.

Today, violence is almost always defined as something aberrant and outside of the norms of culture, and this may or may not hold true for all societies. At best, studies focusing on small-scale societies provide a historically situated snapshot that enables us to expand on how violence is perpetrated and understood from cross-cultural perspectives. Small-scale societies in the past provide us a more nuanced investigation into the emergence and use of violence as an integrated part of cultural behavior. This is often referred to as social violence, or violence that is anticipated, sanctioned, culturally defined, and often featuring elements of both ritual and symbolism. Among human groups it is understood that violence is an ideologically based element of society as well as a strategy that is incorporated into and used within organizational structures. Violent behaviors are therefore deeply embedded within the cultural matrix of societies; to be able to imagine what gender violence was in these early small-scale societies provides insight that contributes to our broader understanding of how and why violence is so entrenched in our species. Humans lived in small-scale societies for thousands of years, so a look at the social behaviors that operated within them provides a baseline for how gender violence got its start, and why it is so ubiquitous today.

Violence among Women

There are contexts where women use nonlethal violence against other women. By examining violence perpetrated by women, Underwood (2003) suggests that violence is a convenient tool in contexts where women seek to dominate other women, which serves to reaffirm social or household status and establishes a hierarchical pecking order within communities, particularly among unrelated women. Martin and Harrod (2015) cited research conducted among a Turkana pastoral community in Kenya that revealed not only domestic violence against women by husbands but also violence between co-wives in the poly-gamous marriages that are the norm within this society. Woman-on-woman violence is a form of gender violence that is less discussed, but a possibility that can become normalized in the same ways as violence perpetrated by men against women.

Bioarchaeological examples of violence between women in the past do exist. Walker (1989) and Lambert (1997) examined skeletal remains from the Channel Islands of southern California (300 BC–AD 1500). The distribution of nonlethal (healed) head wounds men and women exhibited an identical pattern. The fighting that produced these injuries appears to be highly ritualized and performed by adult members of both sexes who were high-status leaders within these groups. Based on grave goods and the location of the burials of these individuals, men and women with nonlethal wounds were treated as high-status individuals in death within this cultural group. Walker (1989) proposed that the combined bioarchaeological and mortuary data suggests ritualized fighting among higher-status men and women. Lambert (1997: 89) suggests that violence among women could also be the result of com-petition among higher-status women. Walker connects ritualized fighting to temporal trends in resource density and an increase in trauma is often seen during periods of low environmental productivity (e.g. droughts). It is possible that these ritualized fights were more for show and public moral than to cause death or disability.

Understanding violence against women and violence perpetrated by women in early small-scale societies is challenging but paying attention to what it would look like in the archaeological record is important.

Documented gender violence between women and between men and women indicates that it has the propensity to become culturally sanctioned and part of everyday behavior, as the examples discussed above suggest. Violence documented among Channel Island groups was more about ritualized battles performed collectively by higher-status men and women than actual conflict or abuse (Lambert, 1997). Among the Turkana, head wounds on men were related to man-on-man violence during warfare and raiding. In contrast, women sustained blows to the head from husbands and other co-wives, offering definitive support for the notion that, like men, women can be the victims of violence, but they also can be perpetrators of it (Harrod et al., 2012).

Violence is an expedient response that often provides results quickly for the person who initiates it. It is also discursive and communicates to witnesses and bystanders messages about power. While everyday interactions among adult men and women include collaborative and cooperative activities, violence can be used to quickly establish a new order or change behaviors that might otherwise be difficult to negotiate through other more peaceful channels. Gender violence in the cases presented here can be seen as a solution to a problem perceived by the perpetrators and sanctioned by their society.

Complexities of Sex and Gender

It is assumed that the cultural perception of biological differences derived from the phenotypic expression of this genetic information over an individual's life course plays a role in the assignment of social responsibilities across sex and age lines (i.e. gender roles). Specifically, individuals expressing what are culturally perceived as variations of "male" and "female" traits at different stages of their biological development will be socialized for particular roles in society, and those roles commonly reflect their assigned genders (Agarwal & Wesp, 2017).

Gender is therefore understood to be a biosocial category distinct from, but related to, biological sex (Zuckerman & Crandall, 2019). It is best conceptualized as a practice, rather than a static state. It is constructed, enacted, and negotiated through the performance of defined social roles, behaviors, and relationships. These are rooted in culturally contingent perceptions and definitions of physiological differences (i.e. sex) at various stages of an individual's ontogeny (i.e. age) (Wesp, 2017).

How can sex and gender be seen in the archaeological record for past cultures? Methodologically, the material correlates of the performance of these roles and their associated practices and behaviors are interpreted in conjunction with age and sex estimates to reflect an individual's gender. The biological manifestations of gender performance used in bioarchaeological analyses include the morphological changes to the skeleton associated with repetitive activities (entheses, robusticity, pathologies, trauma), which are patterned according to age and sex categories (Perry, 2004).

In this volume, gendered terminology such as "woman/women" and "man/men" will be used in discussions of the ethnographic record and what bioarchaeological analyses suggest about the gender that individuals were likely assigned and that structured their lived experience. These skeletal changes and biological categories are often juxtaposed with body arrangement and items included in the mortuary context that are associated with occupational specialization and/or other gendered roles and ideologies based on ethnographic and ethnohistoric analogies (Hollimon, 2017).

The performance of gender, specifically gender roles, produces the material dimensions of gendered lives and identities because they are the practices of men, women, and individuals of nonbinary gender identities in particular social contexts, and these practices often require certain tools and/or produce specific products (Nelson, 2002: 119). As these objects are required for and/or are concomitant with the practice of an individual's gendered role, they contribute to the biomechanical processes that produce the morphological changes to the body/muscles/skeleton through their use and production (Figures 1.3 and 1.4).

In Figure 1.3, there is a depiction of an unmarried young woman grinding corn, which was staged by the photographer circa 1909. While it captures a partial truth about the role of Pueblo women in food production, if this were a more realistic shot, there would be other women next to her grinding, including her mother, sisters, aunts, and grandmother. There would likely be children nearby, and the women would be talking and socializing as they worked. We know this because of the work by Elsie Clews Parsons who lived with and studied Hopi, Zuni and other Pueblo groups with a focus on the various roles of women. Her essays written in the early 1900s were collated into a volume in 1991 (*Pueblo Mothers and Children*) and it provides a rare first-hand account of the daily lives of women and their children. Photographers during that time were under the impression that Native Americans were soon to be extinct, and so there were a number of photographers who traveled around the United States and posed Indigenous people in ways that expressed White notions of who Indians were, i.e., primitive versions of the colonists who had never "progressed" (Egan, 2006).

Figure 1.3 "Hopi maiden grinding corn, Arizona" circa 1909. This depiction
of an unmarried young woman spending hours grinding corn was
staged by the photographer but it does capture a partial truth
about the role of Pueblo women in food production. Public
Domain. Photo courtesy of the United States Library of Congress's
Prints and Photographs Division (digital ID cph 3a51109). http://
hdl.loc.gov/loc.pnp/cph.3a51109.

Because of their facilitation of and association with gendered
practices, everyday utilitarian tools and products demonstrate gendered (and other) identities expressed by and assigned to individuals at
the time of their death by their inclusion in that individual's mortuary
context (Barker, 2017). As an example, many pre-contact Pueblo
women were buried with pieces of pottery and tools, among various
other items (discussed in more depth in Chapter 3). By correlating
suites of burial accompaniments and other mortuary treatments of the
body (i.e. burial location, body positioning, orientation) with skeletal
indicators of activity and juxtaposing these collectively with morpho-
logically identifiable age and sex categories, researchers can interpret
where, when, and how cultures marked and sanctioned gender categories (Hollimon, 2017).

In Figure 1.4, a Hopi woman has been arranged by a photographer
to have the presumed tools of her gender encircling her. From the left
is her grinding stone for processing maize, her utilitarian bowl, a

Figure 1.4 "Moki Indian woman making pottery" 1900/1909. This Hopi woman has been arranged to have the tools of her gender encircling her. Public Domain. Courtesy of Newberry Library, Chicago. Curt Teich Postcard Archives Collection. https://commons.wikimedia.org/w/index.php?curid=67016192.

striped water jug, and a more ceremonial painted bowl. Finally, two cook pots complete her gendered tool kit. She is seen making pottery with her hands using the coil method. Thus, this one staged photo communicates all the important domains in this woman's expected roles—food processing and cooking, meal preparation, collecting water, attending ceremonies, and making pottery. While the date and photographer are no longer known, it appears that this photograph was made into a postcard, likely sold to early tourists from the East who ventured West to see the Indians before they "vanished."

Life Course Theory

The life-course theory has broadened bioarchaeology's approach to the study of sex and gender by recognizing the intersectionality of gender with multiple dimensions of an individual's biological and social identity (e.g. age, class, ethnicity, etc.) in structuring lived experience. Figure 1.5 illustrates the various aspects of expected roles and behaviors that get scripted by the culture. These include biological aspects of age and sex, social aspects of status, class, wealth, and

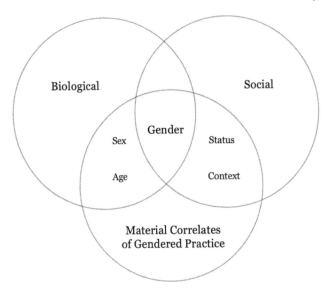

Figure 1.5 Diagram depicting the overlapping axes of gender identity used to reconstruct gender in bioarchaeological and archaeological analyses.

identity, and the tools and "stuff" that become associated with one gender or the others. This shows both how constructed and real gender is, as well as how relational and liminal it is. For example, Agarwal (2012) argues that an individual's gender changes over the life course because their physiological expression and experience of biological sex changes over the life course, particularly for women (e.g. menarche, parturition, menopause), and also for men.

Gender is also relational, meaning it may look different depending on if a woman is among other mothers and wives, or with sisters or brothers, or with parents and grandparents, or with friends and peers. Furthermore, status crosscuts all of these relational associations in that the performance and utilization of specific tools or cultural items are different depending on wealth, kinship relations, and power dynamics. A woman captured and forced to do hard labor will have a very different identity than the woman to whom the captive must subordinate to. Thus, gender sits at the cross-roads of many different intersecting factors that must be considered in order to understand where, when, and how gender violence is used to either submit to or in resistance to constraining social forces.

This idea is best illustrated by the ways in which societies mark particular developmental or social milestones with rites of passage that mark an individual's transition from one social role and its associated responsibilities to another. Ethnographic and ethnohistoric accounts document some of the ways in which physiological stages (i.e. menses) or rites of passage that visually and socially mark gender categories and identities that broadly map onto developmental stages throughout an individual's ontogeny and senescence. For example, according to ethnographic sources, after women reach their first menses among Puebloan groups, their hair is styled into Butterfly Whorls to signify their transition into marriageable status (Figures 1.3 and 1.6) (Parsons, 1936; 1939). After marriage, women arrange their hair in simple plaits (Figures 1.4 and 1.6).

Since it is assumed that gender roles are broadly derived from the perception of the physical characteristics of development and the manifestation of biological sex, then as the physical characteristics of sex change over the life course, so do gender and its expected behaviors and practices. This extends to the consequential risks for experiences of health, disease, and violence that could result from these behaviors and practices, which is important for understanding the patterning of differential experiences of labor, disease, health, and trauma between different age categories of members of the same biological sex.

Intersectionality

Intersectionality theory asserts that categories of social identity, particularly marginalizing identities such as sex, age, gender, race, and class, are not independent but overlap and interact within sociopolitical systems of structural inequality to collectively produce and promote disparities. These disparities are manifested in differential access to necessary resources such as food, shelter, and protection, and the result is the creation of a subgroup placed dangerously at risk for poor health and early death (Yaussy, 2019: 118).

Recent studies by Agarwal (2017), Zuckerman (2017), and Yaussy (2019) utilize an intersectional approach to demonstrate that an individual's identity and lived experience are shaped not only by sex and age, but that these factors are intersectional with other social processes such as gender, socioeconomic status, and life history in promoting or protecting against differential health outcomes (Figure 1.7). In this diagram, intersecting axes of individual experience are shaped by gender as well as age, biological sex, life history, and social status. All of these features of the individual experience are shaped by social interactions and the overall environmental context within which individuals are born into and grow up.

Figure 1.6 "Hopi Indian woman and her daughter in the village of Oraibi circa 1901." The daughter (on the left) is wearing her hair up in two rolls on each side of her head in the Butterfly Whorl style. The mother (on the right) is wearing her hair down in two rolls. Photographers: Charles C. Pierce (1861–1946) & James George Wharton. Source: University of Southern California Libraries and the California Historical Society. Public Domain. http://digitallibrary.usc.edu/cdm/ref/collection/p15799coll65/id/15471 and https://commons.wikimedia.org/w/index.php?curid=30830754.

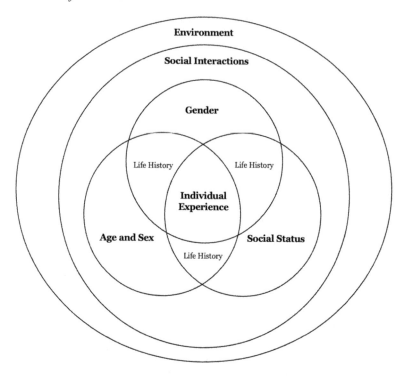

Figure 1.7 Diagram depicting the intersecting axes of identity that interact to shape individual experience.

As an example, Agarwal (2017)'s analysis of the distribution of osteoporosis in the Neolithic population living at Çatalhöyük (74000–6000 BCE) showed that age, rather than sex, was the significant variable structuring disparate risks for experiences of osteoporosis in this population. She argues that the standard practice of segregating skeletal collections into male and female categories as the first step of bioarchaeological analysis obscures the role and relative importance of other axes of social difference in structuring disease experience. Her analysis is significant in that it demonstrates that sex, when considered simultaneously in relation to other axes of differentiation (i.e. age), is not always the most critical social dimension along which differential experience manifests.

Zuckerman (2017) interrogates the relationship between sex, gender, and socioeconomic status as they relate to disease experience and access to medical treatment for acquired syphilis in 17th–18th century London. Specifically, she explored whether the social dimensions of sex and socioeconomic status, as intercorrelated dimensions of gender identity, interacted to prevent women from gaining access to health-care, as suggested by historical sources. She found that there were no sex or status-based differences in skeletal evidence for use of mercury as a treatment for acquired syphilis. Zuckerman interprets this to suggest that poor women found ways around the social systems pre-venting them from accessing treatment to seek healthcare not docu-mented in historical texts. Her study highlights how the different dimensions of gender identity, like sex and socioeconomic status, variably intersect within social systems of inequality to structure within-sex differences of disease experience and opportunities for ex-erting agency.

Finally, Yaussy (2019) identifies the variable associations between age, sex, socioeconomic status, and indicators of physiological stress that influenced and explain differential patterns of frailty and mor-tality in industrializing England between the 18th and 19th centuries. Her study empirically demonstrates how privileging and marginalizing axes of identity during this time period intersected in different contexts to buffer or predispose individuals to negative health outcomes. For example, she posits that high socioeconomic women were buffered against developing lesions through their privileged status, but that same status in younger age categories may have predisposed this group to a higher risk for mortality from childbirth. Yaussy's study is no-teworthy in that it underscores the complex ways different axes of social identity are associated with previous lived experiences of poor health in structuring differential health outcomes within inequitable social systems.

Collectively, these studies illustrate the utility of an intersectional approach in bioarchaeological analyses for clarifying the relative in-fluences of different axes of gender identity (i.e. sex, age, status) and how they interact within social systems of influence and power to structure differential experiences of health within and between groups. They also highlight how gender is a dialectically relational social construct that is as dynamic and fluid as the social relationships and interactions wherein it is defined, negotiated, and enacted. As a result, it is inherently nonbinary and dynamic.

Nonbinary Genders

According to ethnographic and ethnohistoric sources, nonbinary genders in Native North American societies have significant time depth and can be identified archaeologically and bioarchaeologically with careful, contextualized analyses (Hollimon, 2001a). Hollimon (2017) discusses the expression of third and fourth gender identities as they can be identified through archaeological and bioarchaeological analyses. She indicates that third genders are expressed by individuals who are biologically male but do not perform the culturally specific roles traditionally assigned to men nor are they recognized as men in their society (Figure 1.8). This photograph of We-Wha has been used in many explorations of cross-cultural depictions of third sexes. We-Wha was an A:shwi (Zuni) *lhamana* ("man-woman" Basaldu, 1999: 107; "mediating spirit" Hopcke, 2002: 176) individual (circa 1871–1907) who was biologically male, but presented as a woman. Indigenous people today have been identifying as two-spirit for many years and have been reclaiming traditional Indigenous gender categories that include a range of nonbinary expressions of gender. Robinson (2019) shows how shifts in gender frameworks being adopted today are borrowing traditional and contemporary understandings of gender from their ancestors. These reclamations support resistance to ongoing settler colonialism in which every person is male or female.

Similarly, fourth gender is expressed by individuals who are biologically female but do not perform the culturally specific roles traditionally assigned to women and are not recognized as such within their society (Hollimon, 2017: 57). It is important to point out that Native North American gender systems conceptualize, construct, and define gender identities from traits more specific to the individual, like temperament and/or preference and skill for a task (in addition to other attributes), rather than biological sex characteristics, but not necessarily to their exclusion (Goulet, 1996; Hollimon, 2017: 57; Parsons, 1939: 38; Robinson, 2019). Consequently, many Native North American societies have three, four, five or more gender identities.

Although some of the traits determining third and fourth (and other) gender identities may not be visible archaeologically and bioarchaeologically, the physical correlates of the practice and performance of these gender identities can be recovered from the mortuary context and their manifestation as activity markers and trauma on the bones of individuals. For instance, Hollimon (1997) identified potential third-gender males among pre-contact Chumash cultural groups living along coastal California by correlating the distribution of trauma, biomechanical indicators of repetitive activities (i.e. entheses/musculoskeletal stress markers), and degenerative changes at joint complexes with age and sex categories and mortuary treatment. When she contextualized the body/skeletal data, she noted patterns of

Figure 1.8 Photograph of We-Wha, a Zuni lhamana circa 1871–1907. Public
Domain. Photographer: John K. Hillers (1843–1925). Source: U.S.
National Archives and Records Administration (NAID: 523798),
via Wikimedia Commons.

activity markers, degenerative conditions, and traumatic injuries that were more statistically correlated with certain age and sex categories and mortuary treatments, and that there were individuals who exhibited patterns more consistent with individuals of another sex.

As another example, among the ancestral Chumash, Hollimon (1997) identified two young adult male burials that exhibited patterned degenerative changes to their spines that were more commonly observed in older adult females, suggesting that they may have been undertaking similar repetitive physical activities. Included within these men's mortuary context were grave-goods ethnographically consistent with an occupational specialization as undertakers, or individuals who were responsible for handling and burying the dead. Ethnographic and ethnohistoric accounts indicate that this occupation was generally undertaken by third-gender males and postmenopausal women. Therefore, given the combined osteological, mortuary, and ethnographic data, Hollimon (1997) posited that these burials likely reflected third-gender individuals.

Additionally, Hollimon (2001b) identified possible fourth-gender females among Protohistoric Northern Plains Arikara populations who exhibited traumatic injury distributions more commonly associated with young adult men who participated in organized interpersonal conflict. Due to these individuals' injury distributions as well as ethnographic and ethnohistoric analogs from Plains groups, Hollimon (2001b) posited that these individuals may have been warriors who represented fourth-gender individuals. It is important to note however, that inconsistent or nonnormative patterns of biomechanical stress and trauma may not necessarily indicate that a particular cultural group recognizes third or fourth gender identities. Women can periodically engage in interpersonal conflict or even hold warrior status, but that does not necessarily mean that these individuals did not culturally identify as women or were recognized and treated as such by their society (Hollimon, 2017). Therefore, bioarchaeological investigations on nonbinary gender identities in the past must necessarily incorporate multiple lines of evidence, particularly ethnographic/ethnohistoric resources and representational motifs from ceramics, rock-art, figurines, and other mediums in addition to osteological and mortuary contexts.

Agency

Gender is a particularly sensitive lens for exploring differential experiences of stress, manifesting skeletally as variable patterns of morbidity, mortality, and trauma among subgroups, because gender is a principal structuring element in social structures that both limits and promotes opportunities for action within the social practices of daily life (Gero & Conkey, 1991: 9). Giddens' (1984) structuration theory suggests that individuals strategically exert their agency (e.g. take social action) using a referential framework that is composed of the contextually contingent social rules and available materials (e.g. food, land, material goods) and immaterial (e.g. knowledge) resources within a given social system to achieve specific goals (Giddens, 1984: 377). The structure here refers to the set of social rules and available resources that inform, constrain, and enable individual agency. Individual agency is the specific choices and actions people make based on their *capability* to make and act out those decisions within a structure, but with the knowledge that they have the power to decide and act differently. Individual agency is structured and informed by one's own *habitus*, which, according to Bourdieu (1977), is an individual's conceptual and referential framework acquired over a lifetime of being raised (socialized) within a particular social and cultural situation, which conditions (but does not determine) the choices an individual will make in response to specific circumstances.

Gender, therefore, is a structuring principle in that it structures the way an individual negotiates social relationships based on their socialized knowledge of acceptable social mores, which can both limit and promote opportunities for individual action within the social practices of daily life (Zuckerman, 2017). The perceptive frameworks driving the assignment and practice of gender generate behavioral rules that structure social interactions and the organization of daily activities and can also constrain the agency of individuals within any given society. In some circumstances, the restriction of possibilities for action through institutionalized social (gender) roles and their concomitant access to social power and agency manifest skeletally with respect to differential risk for disease, increased workloads, and injury, and experiences of violence within and between age and sex/gender categories (Vésteinsson et al., 2019). If structure informs individual agency and agency is action, and action can be inscribed on the skeleton; then the nature of social power in a given society can be interpreted from the manifestations of its lived experience in skeletal remains (Perry, 2004).

Challenges to Decolonizing the Past

Anyone working as a bioarchaeologist must engage with several important ethical issues regarding working with ancestral bodies/

skeletons. The passage of the Native American Graves Protection and Repatriation Act of 1990 (25 U.S.C. §3001) changed forever the relationships and behaviors of anthropologists who study ancestral human remains and the descendants of those ancestors living today. This legislation mandates that Native American descendants be involved in the decisions made about if and how bodies/skeletons are studied. Permissions must be granted through a chain of local, state, and federal mandates. Individual burials that were excavated prior to this legislation still fall under it, so to analyze ancestral human remains include a series of proposals, consultations, permissions, and requirements that must be carried out with appropriate state and federal offices and Native American representatives.

While there is no monolithic response to requests to analyze Indigenous burials within the United States, tribal representatives will often permit observational analyses where the remains are not altered, dissected, or damaged in any way. On rare occasions, groups may prohibit researchers from doing studies on their ancestors. In our experience, Indigenous people prefer that their ancestors were never disturbed and excavated in the first place, but for older collections housed in repositories, they will often give permission to analyze the bodies if they feel the research questions are of importance to them.

Dr. Rina Swentzell, a Santa Clara Pueblo scholar and architect, had this to say about her ancestors:

> the old ones did not live according to an elaborate and formalized ideology of absolute truth … they lived knowing that this place, this time, is all that there is. This place is where it all happens – happiness, sadness, pain, obligation, responsibility, and joy. (1993: 141)

It is incumbent upon non-Indigenous scholars to recognize and resist their biases and seek ways to decolonize their perceptions, interpretations, and most importantly their articulations of the past, present, and Indigenous lives in particular (D'Arcangelis, 2018). Decolonizing the monopoly of settler-colonial narratives about Indigenous past histories can only be accomplished by collaborating, citing, and consulting with Indigenous representatives and engaging with Indigenous scholarship (see Barnett, 2015; Hargreaves, 2017).

At the most basic level, the data we choose to collect and the way in which we categorize and interpret it to answer specific questions can be biased by our own personal cultural norms and referential frameworks (i.e. a Western biomedical framework), particularly when we categorize bodies/skeletonized remains as being either male or female to the exclusion of other potential sexes, and therefore more varied genders (Geller, 2009). By approaching the division of labor, for example, with the assumption that sex was the most important social category structuring that practice, Geller (2009) argues that researchers may impose Western, binary, biomedical perceptions of sex, gender, and gender roles onto past peoples that may not reflect the reality of their lived experience within their own temporal, cultural, historical, and socio-political context.

The dangers of this approach are that it not only obscures the roles and effects of other categories of social identity in structuring patterns of behavior and experiences of disease and trauma in the past, but that it can essentialize Western notions of sex, gender, and gender roles as inherent or natural to the human species by "identifying" such practices in antiquity (Hager, 1997: 3). This practice has been, and continues to be, used to justify sex and gender-based inequalities in social institutions because it reifies the Western, binary biomedical narratives of sex, gender, and their associated biological expectations and relations that contribute to gendered disparities in health outcomes. To address this, Geller (2008) and Agarwal (2012) suggest that bioarchaeologists shall not estimate osteological sex as a first step toward skeletal analyses, but instead see if one can identify differential patterns of health, disease, workload, or trauma among subgroups and see whether other structuring principles, such as age or class or race, have more of a role in structuring those patterns than biological sex.

Critically consulting ethnographic and ethnohistorical accounts is another avenue toward incorporating Indigenous voices, albeit indirectly. Ethnographic and ethnohistoric resources are invaluable sources of information about the practices and behaviors of everyday life for historic Pueblo peoples that contribute to the holistic body of data archaeologists and bioarchaeologists have traditionally and extensively consulted to reconstruct human behavior, lived experiences, and their material and biological correlates in the past. Ethnographic and ethnohistoric analogy, however valuable, must also be accessed with caution, particularly with respect to sex and gender roles.

Many ethnographic and ethnohistoric sources offer detailed descriptions of aspects of architectural layout and material culture, personal life, the nature of the role and function of secular government and social organization, and aspects of ceremonialism and ritual within the diverse, continuously occupied Pueblos across the American Southwest during the late 19th and 20th centuries. Generally (with some individual or topic-specific deviations), these resources offer brief historical synopses of the Pueblo discussed and their relation to other cultural groups, and offer impressions of the attitudes, behaviors, and practices and beliefs of the people living there.

These descriptions, and associated photos, are useful analogs for understanding how pueblo houses may have generally looked (especially the two storied and multistoried varieties) and what activities took place in particular rooms, which can be connected to archaeological materials. Descriptions of the activities and tools associated with agriculture, horticulture, hunting, war, domesticated animals, pottery-making and crafting, and meal preparation and consumption are all invaluable resources that may have archaeological analogs which researchers can identify and interpret. Although the tools associated with many of these practices during the periods wherein these observations were recorded have been altered through contact with the Spanish and Euro-Americans (e.g. horses, cows, plows, grinding mills) and therefore may not have archaeological correlates, the gender roles associated with some of these tasks could give archaeologists an idea of approximately how labor may have been divided and conservatively how these practices may have been enacted in the past.

Some aspects of everyday life documented in these resources, however, may not have empirically documentable correlates. For instance, ethnographic and ethnohistoric documentations of aspects of personal life like kinship or gender terminology, naming practices, courtship and marriage practices, rules governing house and land ownership, rules governing kiva-membership, initiation rituals, and the practices and informing ideologies of various ceremonies and dances may not have direct archaeological correlates that have utility for analogies. While the descriptions of courtship and marriage, house-ownership, and kiva membership practices could potentially be used to suggest antecedent practices dictating mate choice, household composition (single versus extended family occupation), and kiva-society organization in past communities, testing and documenting these empirically in the archaeological record is challenging. Additionally, descriptions of the various ceremonies that ethnographers and ethnohistorians were allowed to witness, which occasionally included documentation of the time of year, time of day, and what kiva societies were associated with specific ceremonies, could give archaeologists an idea of how integrated community ceremony and ritual may have been practiced and how the architecture of the pueblo (e.g. plazas, kivas) and landscape factored into the performance of these practices in prehistory.

There are several issues with ethnographic and ethnohistoric resources that can limit their utility as appropriate analogies for

Ancestral Pueblos in the American Southwest. Many of the historic period pueblos observed and described in these resources had been, to varying degrees, under the colonial thumb of Spanish and Catholic Church institutions while simultaneously existing within a sphere of interaction between numerous Euro-American, Mexican, and other native Plains culture groups' (e.g. Apache) settlements in the centuries following European contact that were not present in the past. Therefore, the social and material culture of these Pueblos would have been significantly and unavoidably impacted by these interactions through time and the prehistoric antecedents to the observed social structures, behaviors, and practices altered, obscured, or replaced by European models. Therefore, most of these ethnographic documentations are likely to serve as poor analogs for the communities and their daily lives.

Another significant issue limiting the utility of ethnographic and ethnohistoric analogies is the secretiveness of informants, particularly with respect to the ceremonial and ritual practices within the Pueblos, most of which the researcher was not permitted to witness or obtain a complete account of. It should be noted here too, that the sex and gender of the ethnographer also played a role in what types of information and contexts of practice they were privy to within the community they were documenting. The secrecy, as explained to the woman ethnographer Dr. Elise Clews Parsons by one of her informants living within Taos Pueblo of New Mexico, stems from the fear that "Our ways would lose their power if they were known" (Parsons, 1936: 15). She elaborates more on this fear by pointing out that among the people of Taos Pueblo she observed, there was a pervasive association of danger with giving information to the White Man, particularly that this behavior will bring misfortune, sickness, hardship, and even death to the informant (Parsons, 1936: 15). Furthermore, Parsons notes that previous visits to Taos Pueblo by other White people have fomented a mistrust and reluctance of the pueblo community to host other White people. Parsons also notes inconsistencies in the information given to her by her informants, an occasional tendency to indulge White people with half-truths or fabricated folklore, or "camouflaging" certain activities by describing them as something else to protect them (Parsons, 1936: 117).

Finally, language barriers and misconceptions of terminology and philosophy between the researchers and their informants can obscure the true function or meaning of certain facets of life within Pueblo communities (see Goulet, 1996). As an example, an apparent language barrier or misconception of terminology between Dr. Elise Clews

Parsons and her informants was made evident when she attempted to enquire about the "clans" at Taos. Her informant and other towns-people equated the English term "clan" with a ceremonial group (ceremonial society), and subsequently refused to provide any information on the subject. Parsons interpreted this to mean that Taos lacked a clan system, at least in the way the term is applied to some of the social organizations of the western Pueblos. As Taos Pueblo deviates from this pattern in its emphasis on a ceremonial system of kiva society membership, Parsons interprets this to mean that Taos deviates from the "norm" rather than represents a variation on a theme. This interpretation is potentially problematic in that it reveals her presumption that all Pueblos tend to follow a standard (western) Pueblo pattern, which may result in her misunderstanding the social mechanisms she observed. This interpretation is potentially problematic in that it reveals her presumption that all Pueblos tend to follow a standard (western) Pueblo pattern, which may result in her misunderstanding the social mechanisms she observes.

In terms of the utility of ethnographic analogy in general, the issues inherent with any ethnography/ethnohistory do not necessarily preclude its use, but rather speak to the *way* in which ethnographic analogy should be used by archaeologists probing archaeological data. Ware (1999: 139) points out that "to reconstruct the trajectory of a thrown ball, it is just as important to know where the ball lands as to know from where it was thrown." Meaning, instead of using ethnography as a *direct* analog for the archaeological past, it would be better utilized as a tool for identifying and understanding the sources, trajectories, and modes of culture change in these societies through time to illuminate how they may have been and how that contributed to how they are in historic and modern times (Ware, 2014: 15).

Another pathway toward decolonizing anthropological narratives of the past and including Indigenous voices in those reconstructions is to incorporate Indigenous scholarship and oral tradition into interpretations of archaeological data (Dunbar-Ortiz, 2014; Mihesuah, 2003; Windchief & San Pedro, 2019). Oral traditions represent the collective, accumulated knowledge and experiences of generations and how they adapted to and modified their ecological, sociocultural, and political environments to survive through time (Murray & Benitez, 2020). Oral traditions not only provide a mechanism through which history, cultural knowledge, and social institutions are transmitted between generations, but they also inherently embody Indigenous groups' fundamental logics and perceptions of their place in the world and the practices that facilitate their engagement with the environment. In this way, oral traditions influence the way that people perceive and negotiate their physical and social worlds, which consequently affects their behaviors, social mores, and the environment within which these interactions take place (Murray & Benitez, 2020: 5). As such, they can be an invaluable resource for constructing narratives of the past that reflect the realities and logics shaping the lived experiences of individuals that cannot be recovered from their bodies and material culture. Incorporating Indigenous scholarship and oral traditions into anthropological analyses and interpretation will only enhance our understanding of the meanings of human behavior in ways that will more closely reflect the realities of the populations we study and transform the way we comprehend the past and the people who lived there.

Mindful Bodies: Theoretical Framework

Bodies are truth-tellers. Written documents and eyewitness accounts are easily skewed. Archaeologists can reconstruct what kinds of crops people living in the deep past grew, the kinds of animals they hunted, the shape of their habitation areas, and the places where their fires burned. But none of that tells us what people actually ate, whether their shelters were safe spaces, or if individuals were included or excluded from sitting around the hearth. Human skeletal remains (as proxies for bodies and individuals) are truth-tellers because the kinds of pathology and trauma we can observe on their heads, teeth, back, ribs, arms, legs, fingers, and toes reveal many clues into what their daily life was like. The body gives clues to what they ate. The body reveals whether they were beaten. The body divulges how hard they worked on a daily basis. Finally, the body expresses their inclusiveness or marginality in their society.

Our methods of analysis for bodies/skeletons stem from interdisciplinary techniques derived from forensics, archaeology, biology, medicine, clinical studies, anatomy, exercise science, biochemistry, dentistry, and cultural studies. Every part of a skeleton provides information and "memories" about the slings and arrows of everyday misfortunes. One area where bones are particularly good at revealing truths/memories is related to violence or trauma, and this includes things like bone fractures, injuries, disabilities, impairments, and other pathologies related to being beaten, forced to work hard, pushed, or punished.

Some diseases and illnesses are caused by human abuse, neglect, and marginalization. Denied access to food resources, the body becomes malnourished which affects every system in the body. Denied potable water or exposed to parasites from contaminated water results in gastrointestinal illnesses and dysentery that can leach minerals and nutrients from the body, causing characteristic lesions and changes on the bones. Individuals forced to work beyond their physiological capacity can show torn and inflamed muscles that leave signatures on the bones they attach to. These memories speak to those trained to see them.

An important theoretical piece about bodies and suffering, *The Mindful Body* by Scheper-Hughes and Lock (1987), provides a useful framework for comprehending the different ways that cultural practices affect bodies depending on age, gender, identity, status, and life history. The authors state that "less has been written about the ways in which preindustrial societies control their populations and institutionalize means for producing docile bodies and pliant minds in the service of some definition of collective stability, health, and social well-being" (Scheper-Hughes & Lock, 1987: 8). These authors provide a fundamental theoretical framework for thinking about the levels of truth that bodies reveal.

The authors theorize that bodies have three physical and metaphysical levels that can be analyzed. The first level is the *individual body* (Figure 1.9). This body/self represents a person's consciousness or awareness of their body and their direct experience of their body, also referred to as phenomenology. This embodied self exists apart from

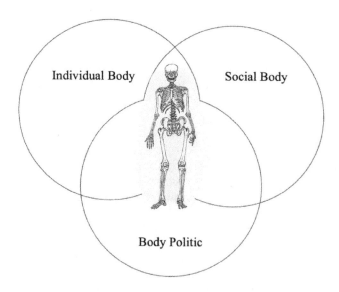

Figure 1.9 Diagram illustrating the Three Bodies Model based on Scheper-Hughes & Lock (1987). Illustration by Claira Ralston.

other individual bodies and is the first-person experience of the world. In other words, how you might view yourself is juxtaposed with how others view you. Depending on cultural context, the individual self may be defined by kinship (daughter, sister, wife, mother), occupation (cook, nanny, farmer, odd jobs), and ethnicity or clan affiliation. These represent basic features of how one sees oneself, but also how one relates to other people.

The individual body is well represented by a range of identifiable diagnostic features on the human skeleton (e.g. age-at-death, osteological sex, gender, musculo-skeletal indicators of labor and work, ethnicity based on burial configuration, clan affiliation based on grave goods, etc.). Thinking about the person-self-body, in societies lacking a highly individualized conception of the body self, sickness is attributed to social relations (such as sorcery/witchcraft), breaking of social moral codes, or to disharmony within the family or community units. For those socialized in Westernized cultures, individualized notions of the self are generally not connected to broader issues of family and community. Rather, illness is perceived to be an individual's problem. Often, individuals are not fully aware of bodies (theirs and/or others) until there is pain and suffering.

The second theorized body is our *social body*. This body is the body as a symbol. What social meanings are ascribed to certain ways the body is presented? As a symbol, the body is simultaneously biological and cultural, and it embodies nearly everything experienced in one's reality. Every detail of bodily presentation and representation symbolizes important relational aspects of an individual's social identity. Social bodies are relational because an individual may be grinding corn and watching over her children which symbolizes motherhood. Or the same individual may be sitting in the sun fixing her younger sister's hair into butterfly whorls symbolizing sisterhood. Or the individual may be taking care of ill parents symbolizing what it means to be a good daughter.

The social body moves fluidly from one axis of identity to another within days or seasons or major life history milestones as the situation and social context dictates. Additionally, there are life history moments that transform the social body, including menstruation, sexual activities, marriage, pregnancy, motherhood, working outside the home, and menopause. The social body is often modified and decorated in ways that communicate a social identity. Social bodies make a statement to others about who they are. Clothing, body painting, hair styling, facial makeup, tattoos, jewelry, and the way parts of the body are exposed or hidden, all communicate the social identity of the person. In addition to this, body modifications in the form of piercings, scarification, head shaping, dental modifications (filing, fillings, creation of spaces and designs), and transformations in foot size or neck length are more intensive ways to use the social body to communicate identity as well as belonging. All of these are the means through which the individual body self-identifies, is shaped, constructed, and presented, and ultimately the way that it is identified and interpreted within the socially specific cultural milieu.

The third theorized body is the *body politic*. This refers to the ways that bodies are constrained and shaped to be useful for sustaining a particular set of societal relations. The *body politic* asks in what ways are bodies under surveillance or regulation? How are bodies socialized for societal needs? The *body politic* is often about the contentious control of bodies by powerful outside forces, both individual and collective. The objectification of some bodies and not others or the way that bodies are commodified, constrained and/or punished as part of social and political control reveal the often-dark side of living within societies with rules that govern which bodies are safe from harm, and which bodies can be harmed. The politically constrained body, or in this sense the politically *correct* body, can entail distortions of human anatomy. For example. Stone and Sanders (2020) elucidate and complicate the *body politic* of Victorian women's bodies and the symbolism, embodiment, and resistance of the corseted body, and how it shaped female health and identity in the 19th century. Chinese foot binding was a practice to distinguish the higher class from lower class women. Women thought to be witches were punished in particular ways during colonial periods in America.

Scheper-Hugh's and Lock (1987)'s concept of a mindful body is a complex way to think about gender and bodies. The heuristic device that they use involving the three bodies helps to organize the various ways that bodies respond to and are shaped by societal forces. Using the three bodies helps to problematize human bodies which are often analyzed in a straightforward descriptive manner that does not permit a deeper interpretation of the meaning of the lesions, diseases, and trauma written on the body/skeletons. A standard bioarchaeological analysis of a skeleton might reveal that a person was a 35-year-old female with a healed broken arm and markers of malnutrition who was buried with several cooking pots. Using the three-bodies approach invites a deeper and more nuanced probing of other sources of information on that individual that would provide a way to access the social body as well as the body politic. Trauma, disease, and disability are not isolated random acts, but patterned, produced, and embedded within a complex network of interactions between the individual body, the social relations of the person within the community, and the political processes which govern how bodies are viewed and treated.

Summary

While the descendants of the community discussed in this volume are here today and living in Pueblo towns up and down the Rio Grande River in New Mexico as well is at Hopi and Zuni in Arizona, they surely have their own stories and explanations about their past. This study is not to replace what Indigenous women have to say about their counterparts in the past. Our scientific and empirically based work through bioarchaeological methods presented here is but one of many stories that exist about the Pueblo past. As White researchers, the story we tell here is more empirical and based on reading the bodies, but our interpretations may fall short of being absolute or the only way to see things.

We are hopeful that the truth-telling we do from reading the bones of women who perished in the past is useful in providing a longer arc of understanding about gender violence writ large. Yet we acknowledge that no one asked us to study these particular ancestors and so we must bear the burden of having some Pueblo people today who would have preferred that we not study these ancestors. As we discuss in Chapter 2, all appropriate channels were attended to in obtaining permission to study these ancestors 25 years ago, and the data we draw on here was eventually published in a descriptive report (Martin et al., 2001). As scientists who wish to understand the actual experiences of women who are abused, we feel it is important. But as Leslie Marmon Silko, a Pueblo novelist and poet, has written, quoting Gabriel García Márquez (https://www.nobelprize.org/prizes/literature/1982/marquez/lecture)—"The interpretation of our reality through patterns not our own serves only to make us ever more unknown, ever less free, ever more solitary." This clear sense of violation by the study of Pueblo ancestors by outsiders may be offset with this quote from Ned Blackhawk (2006: 5–6) who writes—"Violence becomes more than an intriguing or distressing historical subject. It becomes an interpretive concept as well as a method for understanding these understudied worlds." We believe that violence against women is an "understudied world" and we hope to contribute to shining a light on its ubiquity and persistence across both time and different cultures.

Social theories such as the one presented here by Scheper-Hughes and Lock (1987) are frameworks that focus our attention on particular facets of human social interactions, organizations, and behaviors

(Powers, 2010: 5). Bioarchaeology relies on the biocultural approach to facilitate the integration of data from human remains (biology) with other archaeological data from every aspect of lived experience that produces the material dimensions of daily life, including pottery (food preparation and storage), housing (shelter and organization space), faunal and plant remains (food cultivation, domestication, and consumption), weapons (hunting, social competition, and conflict), tools and hearths (resource production, crafts), to name a few of the datasets we rely on for context. Using these multidimensional datasets for reconstructing past lives, social theory enhances our interpretations of the past. Social theories help us identify and flesh out the larger political and economic structures that affect daily experiences and the behaviors that produce the material dimensions of lived experience, and consequently those that impact general health and well-being over long periods of time. Social theories also facilitate our capacity to formulate causal relationships that explain when, how and why certain events in human history occurred.

The kind of bioarchaeological study presented in this volume provides intimate portraits of lived experiences that span the course of individuals' lives, providing snapshots of daily, seasonal, annual, and generational aspects of the human experience. Life course theory provides bioarchaeologists with insights into diet, health, injury, growth, maintenance, and reproductive functions because skeletal assemblages often include individuals of both sexes who died at varying ages. In addition, bioarchaeological data also provides information at multiscalar levels so that groups can be examined at the individual, community, regional, and interregional levels. As a subdiscipline within anthropology, bioarchaeology focuses on cross-cultural comparisons of humans in varied and distinctive settings focusing, for example, on different subsistence economies, different political structures, or contrasting environmental settings. Even when there are written documents, the human remains and associated archaeological contexts often reveal a more nuanced, detailed, and authentic account of what social life was really like for individuals and groups.

Therefore, bioarchaeological data is vitally important when thinking about the past because of its added value in substantiating biological and cultural dynamics. The data derived from the bodies of people long gone cannot speak for themselves. Interpretations of bioarchaeological data rely heavily on the judicious use of social theories. Integrating bioarchaeological data with social theory is important because the stakes are high. The world is a full of troubles and problems for which there are no easy answers. Bioarchaeological data reveals ways that humans in the past have survived by accommodating and adapting to diverse forms of stress, from droughts and warfare to the topic of this book, gender violence, captivity, and slavery.

References

Agarwal, S.C. (2012). The past of sex, gender, and health: Bioarchaeology of the aging skeleton. *American Anthropologist*, 114(2), 322–335. DOI:10.1111/j.1548-1433.2012.01428.x.

Agarwal, S. (2017). Understanding sex-and gender-related patterns of bone loss and health in the past: A case study from the Neolithic community of Çatalhöyük. In S.C. Agarwal, and J. Wesp (Eds.), *Exploring sex and gender in bioarchaeology* (pp. 165–188). University of New Mexico Press.

Agarwal, S., & Wesp, J. (2017). *Exploring sex and gender in bioarchaeology*. University of New Mexico Press.

Barker, C.S. (2017). Inconspicuous identity: Using corrugated pottery to explore social identity within the Homol'ovi settlement cluster, A.D. 1260-1400. (Doctoral Dissertation, University of Arizona). https://www.proquest.com/docview/1983517795?pq-origsite=gscholar&fromopenview=true.

Barnett, K.D. (2015). Indigenous feminist approaches to archaeology: Building a framework for indigenous research in pre-colonial archaeology. (Doctoral Dissertation, University of Montana). https://www.proquest.com/docview/1734104605?pq-origsite=gscholar&fromopenview=true.

Basaldu, R.C. (1999). *Hopi hova: Anthropological assumptions of gendered otherness in Native American societies*. (Masters' Thesis, The University of Arizona). https://www.proquest.com/docview/220038320?pq-origsite=gscholar&fromopenview=true.

Blackhawk, N. (2006). *Violence over the land: Indians and empires in the early American west*. Harvard University Press.

Bourdieu, P. (1977). *Outline of a theory of practice* (Vol. 16). Cambridge University Press.

Cameron, C.M. (2016). *Captives: How stolen people changed the world*. University of Nebraska Press.

D'Arcangelis, C.L. (2018). Revelations of a white settler woman scholar-activist: The fraught promise of self-reflexivity. *Cultural Studies↔Critical Methodologies*, 18(5), 339–353. 10.1177/1532708617750675.

Dunbar-Ortiz, R. (2014). *An indigenous people's history of the United States*. Beacon Press.

Egan, S. (2006). "Yet in a primitive condition": Edward s. Curtis's North American Indian. *American Art*, 20(3), 58–83. 10.1086/511095.

Galtung, J. (1969). Violence, peace, and peace research. *Journal of Peace Research*, 6(3), 167–191. 10.1177/002234336900600301.

Geller, P.L. (2008). Conceiving sex: Fomenting a feminist bioarchaeology. *Journal of Social Archaeology*, 8(1), 113–138. 10.1177/1469605307086080.

Geller P.L. (2009). Identity and difference: Complicating gender in archaeology. *Annual Review of Anthropology*, 38, 65–81. 10.1146/annurev-anthro-091908-164414.

Gero, J.M., & Conkey, M.W. (Eds) (1991). *Engendering archaeology: Women in prehistory*. Blackwell Publishers Ltd.

Giddens, A. (1984). *The constitution of society: Outline of the theory of structuration*. University of California Press.

Goulet, J.A. (1996). The 'Berdache'/'Two-Spirit:' A comparison of anthropological and native constructions of gendered identities among the Northern Athapaskans. *The Journal of the Royal Anthropological Institute*, 2(4), 683–701. 10.2307/3034303.

Hager, L.D. (1997) Sex and gender in paleoanthropology. In L.D. Hager (Ed.), *Women in human evolution* (pp. 1–28). Routledge.

Hargreaves, A. (2017). *Violence against indigenous women: Literature, activism, resistance*. Wilfrid Laurier University Press.

Harrod, R.P., Liénard, P., & Martin, D.L. (2012). Deciphering violence in past societies: Ethnography and the interpretation of archaeological populations. In D.L. Martin, R.P. Harrod, and V.R. Pérez (Eds.), *The bioarchaeology of violence* (pp. 63–80). University Press of Florida.

Hart, S.M. (2019) *Colonialism, community and heritage in native New England*. University of Florida Press.

Hollimon, S.E. (1997). The third gender in native California: Two-spirit undertakers among the Chumash and their neighbors. In C. Classen, and R.A. Joyce (Eds.), *Women in prehistory: North America and Mesoamerica* (pp. 173–188). University of Pennsylvania Press.

Hollimon, S.E. (2001a). The gendered peopling of North America: Addressing the antiquity of systems of multiple genders. In N. Price (Ed.), *The archaeology of Shamanism*, (pp. 123–134). Psychology Press.

Hollimon, S.E. (2001b). Warfare and gender in the Northern Plains: Osteological evidence of trauma reconsidered. In B.A. Arnold, and N.L. Wicker (Eds.), *Gender and the archaeology of death*, Vol. 2 (pp. 179–193). Rowman Altamira.

Hollimon, S.E. (2017). Bioarchaeological approaches to non-binary genders: Case studies from native North America. In S. Agarwal, and J. Wesp (Eds.), *Exploring sex and gender in bioarchaeology* (pp. 51–70). University of New Mexico Press.

Hopcke, R.H. (2002). *Jung, Jungians and homosexuality*. Wipf and Stock Publishers.

Lambert, Patricia M. (1997). Patterns of violence in prehistoric hunter-gatherer societies of coastal southern California. In D.L. Martin, and D.W. Frayer (Eds.), *Troubled times: Violence and warfare in the past* (pp. 145–180). Amsterdam: Gordon and Breach.

Lonetree, A. (2012). *Decolonizing museums: Representing native America in national and tribal museums*. University of North Carolina Press.

Marek-Martinez, O.V. (2021). Indigenous archaeological approaches and the refusal of colonialism in archaeology. In L.M. Panich, and S.L. Gonzalez (Eds.), *The routledge handbook of the archaeology of indigenous-colonial interaction in the Americas* (pp. 503–515). Routledge. https://doi-org. ezproxy.library.unlv.edu/10.4324/9780429274251

Martin, D.L., Akins, N.J., Goodman, A.H., & Swedlund, A.C. (2001). *Harmony and discord: Bioarchaeology of the La Plata Valley*. Museum of New Mexico Press.

Martin, D.L., & Anderson, C.P. (Eds.) (2014). *Bioarchaeological and forensic perspectives on violence: How violent death is interpreted from skeletal remains*. Cambridge University Press.

Martin, D.L., & Harrod, R.P. (2015). Bioarchaeological contributions to the study of violence. *American Journal of Physical Anthropology*, 156, 116–145.

Martin, D.L., & Harrod, R.P. (2020). Gendered Violence in the Past. In L.L. O'Toole, J.R. Schiffman, and R. Sullivan (Eds.), *Gender violence: Multidisciplinary perspectives* (3rd Edition, pp. 13–24). New York University Press. 10.18574/9781479801794

Martin, D.L., Harrod, R.P., & Pérez, V.R. (Eds.) (2013). *Bioarchaeology: An integrated approach to working with human remains*. Springer. 10.1007/ 978-1-4614-6378-8_1

Mihesuah, D.A. (2003). *Indigenous American women: Decolonization, empowerment, activism*. University of Nebraska Press.

Murray, J.K., & Benitez, R.A. (2020). Weaving environmental knowledge and oral tradition. *Anthropology News* website, October 23, 2020. DOI: 10.145 06/AN.1520.

Nelson, S.M. (2002). Gender Roles. In S.M. Nelson, and M. Rosen-Ayalon (Eds.), *In pursuit of gender: Worldwide archaeological approaches* (pp. 119–124). AltaMira Press.

Panich, L.M., & Gonzalez, S.L. (Eds.) (2021). *The routledge handbook of the archaeology of indigenous-colonial interaction in the Americas*. Routledge.

Parsons, E.W.C. (1936). *Taos Pueblo* (No. 2). George Banta Publishing Company.

Parsons, E.W.C. (1939). *Pueblo Indian religion* (Vol. 1). University of Nebraska Press.

Passalacqua, N.V., Pilloud, M.A., & Gruters, G.A. (2014). Professionalism: Ethics and scholarship in forensic science. *Journal of Forensic Sciences*, 59, 573–575. 10.1111/1556-4029.12433

Perry, E.M. (2004). Bioarchaeology of labor and gender in the prehispanic American Southwest. (Doctoral Dissertation, University of Arizona).

Powers, C.H. (2010). *Making sense of social theory: A practical introduction*. Rowman & Littlefield.

Robinson, M. (2019). Two-spirit identity in a time of gender fluidity. *Journal of Homosexuality*, 67(12), 1675–1690. 10.1080/00918369.2019.1613853.

Scheper-Hughes, N., & Lock, M.M. (1987). The mindful body: A prolegomenon to future work in medical anthropology. *Medical Anthropology Quarterly*, 1(1), 6–41. 10.1525/maq.1987.1.1.02a00020

Sicola, M. (2020). Anti-white supremacist strategies in American Indian art museum exhibitions (Master's Thesis, American University). https://ezproxy.library.arizona.edu/login?url=https://www.proquest.com/dissertations-theses/anti-white-supremacist-strategies-american-indian/docview/2408566273/se-2?accountid=8360.

Squires, K., Roberts, C.A., & Márquez-Grant, N. (2022). Ethical considerations and publishing in human bioarchaeology. *American Journal of Biological Anthropology*, 1–5. DOI: 10.1002/ajpa.24467

Stone, P.K., & Sanders, L.S. (2020). *Bodies and lives in Victorian England: Science, sexuality, and the affliction of being female*. Routledge.

Swentzell, R. (1993). Mountain form, village form: Unity in the Pueblo World. In S.H. Lekson, and R. Swentzell (Eds.), *Ancient land, ancestral places: Paul Logsdon in the Pueblo Southwest* (pp. 139–147). Museum of New Mexico Press.

Tummala-Narra, P. (2020). Intersectionality in the immigrant context. *Intersectionality and relational psychoanalysis: New perspectives on race, gender and sexuality*. In M. Belkin, and C. White (Eds.), *Intersectionality and relational psychoanalysis: New perspectives on race, gender, and sexuality* (pp. 119–143). Routledge.

Thomas, J.-L., & Krupa, K.L. (2021). Bioarchaeological ethics and considerations for the deceased. *Human Rights Quarterly*, 43(2), 344–354. 10.1353/hrq.2021.0022

Trabert, S. (2022). Considering the long-term consequences of designating native American sites as European creations. In T.D. Schneider, and L.M. Panich (Eds.), *Archaeologies of indigenous presence* (1st ed., pp. 89–108). University Press of Florida. 10.2307/j.ctv28m3hb5.10

Underwood, M.K. (2003). *Social aggression among girls*. The Guilford Press.

Vésteinsson, O., Hegmon, M., Arneborg, J., Rice, G., & Russel, W.G. (2019). Dimensions of inequality: Comparing the North Atlantic and the US Southwest. *Journal of Anthropological Archaeology* 54, 172–191. 10.1016/j.jaa.2019.04.004.

Walker, P.L. (1989). Cranial injuries as evidence of violence in prehistoric southern California. *American Journal of Anthropology*, 80(3), 313–323. 10.1002/ajpa.1330800305.

Ware, J.A. (1999). The present as destination: The role of ethnography in prehistoric pueblo research. *Affiliation Conference on Ancestral Peoples of the Four Corners Region*, 5, 134–142.

Ware, J.A. (2014). Ware, J.A. (2014). *A Pueblo social history: Kinship, sodality, and community in the Northern Southwest*. School for Advanced Research Press.

Wesp, J.K. (2017). Embodying sex/gender systems in bioarchaeological research. In (Eds.), *Exploring sex and gender in bioarchaeology* (pp. 99–126). University of New Mexico Press.S. AgarwalJ. Wesp

Wilcox, M., D. Lippert, L.M. Montgomery, LL.J. Zimmerman, G. Nicholas, P.A. McAnany, M. Conkey C. Colwell, R. McGuire (2022) "Does the SAA really listen?" SAA Record 22(2):10–13.

Windchief, S., & San Pedro, T. (Eds.) (2019). *Applying indigenous research methods: Storying with peoples and communities.* Routledge.

Yaussy, S.L. (2019). The intersections of industrialization: Variation in skeletal indicators of frailty by age, sex, and socioeconomic status in 18th-and 19th-century England. *American Journal of Physical Anthropology,* 170, 116–130. 10.1002/ajpa.23881.

Zuckerman, M.K. (2017). Mercury in the midst of Mars and Venus: Reconstructing gender, sexuality, and socioeconomic status in relation to mercury treatment for Syphilis in seventeenth to nineteenth century London. In S. Agarwal, and J. Wesp (Eds.), *Exploring sex and gender in bioarchaeology* (pp. 223–262). University of New Mexico Press.

Zuckerman, M.K., & Crandall, J. (2019). Reconsidering sex and gender in relation to health and disease in bioarchaeology. *Journal of Anthropological Archaeology* 54, 161–171. 10.1016/j.jaa.2019.04.001.

2 Portrait of a Desert Farming Community

Introduction

To better reconstruct and understand the lived experiences (and social roles) of individuals in the deep past we must first place them back into the world they navigated. Therefore, this chapter is a dive into what is currently known about the archaeologically reconstructed environment and cultural systems of the desert-farming communities who lived in the La Plata River Valley throughout the AD 1000s, whose lives we highlight in this volume. It is well established that sedentary farmers, compared to mobile forager-hunter-gatherers, experienced more health problems due to nutritional inadequacies, transmissible infectious diseases, parasites, higher infant mortality, and increased interpersonal conflict, which resulted in trauma and injuries (see Cohen & Armelagos, 1984). The individuals discussed in this volume lived during a time period that archaeologists refer to as the Pueblo II period (AD 900–1150) in the American Southwest.

Most of the individuals recovered during the La Plata Highway Archaeological Project lived around AD 1050–1150. Looking into the broader social and political climate throughout the AD 1100s in the American Southwest provides compelling reasons for concern with respect to women's overall health and experiences of disease and violence. What was going on in general and where did power reside within homes, communities, and regions? To answer this, we look to reconstructions of the archaeological record and to ethnographic sources on traditional women's roles (see Chapter 5). However, before we do so, just like before any bioarchaeological investigation should take place, we must first ask ourselves two crucial questions: Should we study other people's ancestors' bodies (if they are not our own) and why these ancestors' bodies in particular?

DOI: 10.4324/9781003123521-2

Studying Other People's Bodies—Concerns and Caveats

The archaeological research from which the individuals discussed in this volume were encountered was carried out under what is colloquially referred to as *salvage archaeology*. In this case, the sites from which these individuals were recovered were excavated as part of the La Plata Highway Archaeological Project because a road in New Mexico near Farmington needed to be widened to include a shoulder, and the construction of this shoulder would pass through several archaeological sites that would be destroyed as a result. Per law in the United States of America (e.g. National Historic Preservation Act, National Environmental Policy Act, and the Archaeological Resources Protection Act), when land is to be disturbed for construction, a certified team of archaeologists must first assess if there are any relevant ancient, historic or contemporary sites that will be placed at risk by the undertaking. The Museum of New Mexico's Office of Archaeological Studies proposed a plan for excavating the previously identified Pueblo II (AD 900–1100) archaeological sites that would have been destroyed because of the construction of this shoulder along the existing road. However, the provisions of these legal statutes are that the assigned archaeologists can only excavate the areas that will be destroyed by the widening of the road on either side and nothing else.

When burial remains were found among the structures excavated, the Museum of New Mexico's then Acting Director Tim Maxwell contacted the Chairperson of the Sensitive Materials Committee and attached a proposal for how the buried individuals would be respectfully and carefully excavated and analyzed. The letter outlined many observational techniques for acquiring data from the skeletonized bodies that are standardized and used by all bioarchaeologists who work with burials. It was also requested that small pieces of bone be utilized for isotopic analyses to detect and interpret what people were eating. The Sensitive Material Committee Co-Chairs Thomas Livesay and Ed Ladd provisionally approved this proposal for working with the ancestors but cautioned that it also needed to be approved by Herman Agoyo, the then-Chair of the Eight Northern Pueblo Council and Regis Pecos, formerly of the State Office for Indian Affairs. The required permissions were obtained, and the excavation and analyses were carried out in the early 1990s. A full report of all of the analyses was published in a summary volume that can be accessed as a free download at the following link: http://www.nmarchaeology.org/assets/files/archnotes/242.pdf.

However, projects like the La Plata Highway Archaeological Project are tricky and complex in terms of ethics. Just because this project followed all the proper local, state, and national requirements doesn't necessarily mean that descendant groups living in the region approved of the excavation and retrieval of burials and artifacts, or the analyses that followed. Furthermore, it is not clear which tribal entity most affiliates with these individuals. During a repatriation consultation in the 2000s, none of the local tribal representatives requested the remains and associated artifacts be repatriated to their tribe. To be sure, these are ancestral Pueblo people, but perhaps the timing and logistics of returning the ancestors to a new burial ground made claiming these burials difficult.

Should those of us interested in the past for what it reveals about our present and future predicament in terms of women's near universal subordination be permitted to study other people's ancestors? This is a question that we invite readers to think about, and we have no ready answers. Because this particular group of women's remains represents poignant narratives of how gendered violence underwrites pain and suffering for some women, it is important to share their stories more for what they reveal about humans in general, and not explicitly Indigenous women who lived over 1,000 years ago. The descendants of the communities discussed in this volume are alive and well, living in Pueblo towns up and down the Rio Grande River in New Mexico today, and they have their own stories, explanations, and ways of knowing about their past. As discussed in Chapter 1, it is incumbent upon researchers to decolonize their perception of knowledge and ways of knowing about the past.

The first step toward decolonizing knowledge is to reposition Indigenous ways of knowing and scholarship at the center of interpretation (Huff et al., 2020). Leslie Marmon Silko, a Pueblo novelist and poet, highlights the essential significance of oral narratives to Puebloan peoples for the maintenance of their culture, worldview, and survival, stating that the "ancient people perceived the world and themselves within that world as part of an ancient continuous story composed of innumerable bundles of other stories" (Silko, 1987: 87). Decolonizing methodologies do not necessarily require that we must completely reject Western knowledge and research methods, but rather that we must center Indigenous scholarship, worldviews, perceptions, and agendas in the creation of knowledge to interpret the past from an Indigenous perspective (Tuhiwai Smith, 1999). The study discussed in this volume is not presented to replace what Indigenous people, particularly women, know and have to say about their counterparts in the past. Our scientific and empirically based work through bioarchaeological methods is but one of many stories that exist about the past. As White anthropologists, the story we tell here from the biological and material data co-exists with and complements retellings of the past through oral tradition and other narrative modes.

Why a Small-Scale Society?

Desert farmers represent a comparatively short, but exceptionally pivotal moment in the timeline of humanity's tenure on the planet. Recall that humans spent nearly 2 million years surviving as forager-hunter-gatherers, living in small mobile groups and moving about the landscape, following seasonal shifts in the availability of wild floral and faunal resources. It wasn't until the Neolithic Revolution (circa 12,000 years ago) that the shift to cultivation and domestication of cultigens and animals began to emerge and fundamentally change the way humans interacted with their environment and with each other. Prior to the Neolithic Revolution, communicable disease and violence do not appear to have played a significantly large role in daily life, and while life was hard and life expectancy was shorter, bioarchaeological data suggests that forager-hunter-gatherers enjoyed comparatively good health—partly due to the diverse and balanced diet afforded by their subsistence strategies (Zuckerman et al., 2014). The progressive shift to agriculture as the predominant subsistence strategy during the Neolithic and beyond constituted a major demographic and lifestyle shift, with human groups becoming increasingly sedentary and living clustered together for extended periods of time, increasing reliance on a less diverse diet of domesticated grains and legumes, and increasing exposure to old and new parasitic infections and infectious diseases.

For the past 12,000 years or so, this was the configuration for most human groups across the world. It wasn't until the Industrial Revolution in the mid-1700s that there was a second major demographic and lifestyle transition that saw people moving into cities, working in factories, traveling further across the globe than ever before. This transition was also accompanied by the concomitant emergence of infectious diseases that could and did give rise to epidemics and pandemics that still resonate and impact populations today. Therefore, that span of 12,000 years as Neolithic farmers is important to document and understand with respect to the adaptations that people had to make to accommodate these new ways of living.

In the American Southwest, particularly in the region where Colorado, Utah, Arizona, and New Mexico meet (the Four Corners

Region), Indigenous people have lived for thousands of years, first as forager-hunter-gatherers and, starting about 4,000 years ago, as farmers (da Fonseca et al., 2015). These farmers survived numerous climate shifts and changes in unstable and marginalized areas. Furthermore, growing enough food to feed and sustain what was likely a growing population during the AD 1000s in the marginal environment that characterizes this region required ingenuity and cooperation. The successes of these first small-scale societies resonate through the fact that, while Indigenous peoples lived here in the deep past, they still live and thrive there today. The first, and longest inhabitants of the region are ancestral to the Puebloan Peoples, who include as many as twenty different groups, such as the Zuni, Hopi, and the Santa Clara Pueblo. In historic times Navajo people emigrated into the region from the far north, and then during the colonial period, nonIndigenous colonists settled there, along with a mix of Mexican, Spanish, and Anglo settlers.

The small-scale societies that made their livelihoods in the American Southwest are crucial to understand because they represent a baseline for the full range of human experiences with environments, diseases, cultural changes, nutritional challenges, and violence. In desiring to understand when, where, and under what circumstances gendered divisions of labor and power became established, we look to these early small-scale farming communities. Focusing on the Puebloan inhabitants of the La Plata region is important because these people are the original inhabitants of this ostensibly inhospitable landscape. They represent generations of accumulated knowledge and experience of successful adaptations—both economic and social—to the vicissitudes of their marginal ecological and cultural environments. As such, these communities provide a framework for understanding how systems of sociopolitical and economic strategies and relations shaped their daily lives, and how men and women fared under those arrangements.

Bodies in Context: Environments, Cultural Processes, and Biology

Bioarchaeological analyses like the one discussed in this volume, using the lens of a biocultural approach, situate osteological and burial data within their ecological, historical, political, and cultural contexts and interpret these data within the frameworks of social theories to identify extrinsic and intrinsic factors which influenced past human behaviors that left permanent marks on the skeleton (Zuckerman & Martin, 2016). The main premise of a biocultural approach is that humans are simultaneously biological and cultural beings, and the skeleton represents the physical expression of accumulated biological responses to lived (cultural) experiences.

A biocultural model is an analytical tool that facilitates a holistic methodology that draws on multidisciplinary perspectives and methods to identify and interpret the biological correlates of human behavior and to explain that behavior within its broader context. By contextualizing biological data using available ecological, archaeological, ethnohistoric, and historic information, bioarcheologists can reconstruct the cultural and socio-political frameworks within which individuals and groups operated, and identify the sociopolitical institutions and processes promoting and upholding differential patterns of health, disease, labor, and trauma across subgroups (i.e. sex, gender, age, ethnicity) within and between populations (Zuckerman & Martin, 2016).

A visual model (Figure 2.1) provides a generalized framework within which researchers can model physiological stress within its larger context of environmental and cultural factors that prevent or promote stress specific to the problems impacting the populations under investigation.

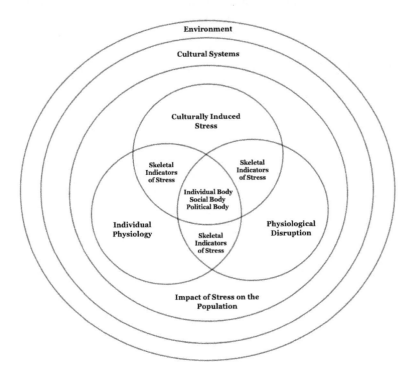

Figure 2.1 Diagram of a general biocultural model of stress.

In this model, the **environment** represents available resources essential for survival (i.e. reliable food resources, access to water, shelter) and includes the constraints on these resources (i.e. marginal environment, unpredictable rainfall, drought) at any given point in time that may limit a population's ability to survive.

Cultural systems like technology, social organization, or ideology act as buffering mechanisms that filter the physical environment to protect individuals during physiologically stressful periods such as weaning, pregnancy, and shifts in ecological conditions, like drought or famine. However, occasionally these cultural buffering systems can introduce additional stressors that promote poor health outcomes. For example, if cultigens were relied on increasingly through time, it would make it difficult to meet dietary requirements in the face of protracted drought conditions and crop failure several years in a row. Ecological and climate stressors would be further exacerbated if population size was simultaneously growing and/or the social groups were invested in rigid adaptive strategies (i.e. hierarchical social arrangements, exclusive focus on agriculture in marginal environments, etc.). On the other hand, increased resource and information sharing, storage capacity, trading, and redistribution of limited resources supplemented with flexibility in resource emphasis and procurement strategies can offset stressors introduced through the use of crop cultivation. Thus, cultural buffering systems like reliance on cultigens can be perceived as both a buffer during ecologically favorable times and a stressor during periods of drought.

Illustrative examples of **culturally-induced stress** include food taboos that limit nutritional intake based on life stages like pregnancy, which may make some otherwise nutritionally beneficial foods off limits to pregnant women, causing nutritional deficiencies that impact the overall health of the mother and consequentially her baby. Marriage patterns also can increase the prevalence of genetic anomalies within a population and/or expose adolescent girls to pregnancies at very young ages (Yaussy, 2019), which could put them at increased risk for early mortality.

The **individual physiology** sphere acknowledges that, due to both biological and cultural differences in the availability of and access to resources and reserves, not all individuals are equally at risk for poor health. Certain segments of the population (i.e. weaning age infants, pregnant & postpartum women, the elderly) may be at greater risk relative to others at certain ages or life stages because their biological requirements are not matched by biological resources like mature and/or healthy and unstressed immune systems. This sphere acknowledges that critical biological factors such as age, sex, health status, genetic composition, and nutritional composition as well as cultural factors like status and wealth can mitigate, moderate, or exacerbate the severity of experiences of different kinds of **physiological disruption** in the face of exposure to environmental and culturally induced disruptions and pathogens.

Experiences of prolonged exposure to stress lead to **physiological disruptions** that can be either beneficial or detrimental to an individual's survival depends on the matrix of circumstances constructed by the combination and interactions of the external **environment, cultural systems**, and **individual physiology** that an individual negotiates at any given time. These physiological disruptions manifest phenotypically, particularly in developing juvenile individuals, but also in developmentally mature individuals that are identifiable and interpretable from skeletal and dental remains (**skeletal indicators of stress**), including growth disruptions and diagnostic skeletal lesions. These can include (but are not limited to) growth stunting (relative adult stature), linear enamel hypoplasias, cribra obitalia, porotic hyperostosis, periosteal reactions, osteoarthritis (OA), and enthesopathies.

While **skeletal indicators of stress** occur at the level of the individual, their incidence and prevalence at the population level (**impact of stress on the population**) have significant consequences for the success (or failure) of cultural buffering systems in mitigating the effects of environmental constraints. Therefore, it is important to consult the clinical manifestations of disease processes to identify their effects at a community level. For instance, groups experiencing poor health and/ or malnutrition may express diminished work capacity, fertility, and life expectancy, which disrupts social, political, and ideological systems to the point of instability. This instability strains systems of cultural support (i.e. cultural buffering systems such as cultivation or agriculture) that usually mitigate the effects of environmental constraints; however, these constraints can be exacerbated by a group's adaptive response to the strain on their cultural buffering system(s) (i.e. ecological degradation due to agricultural intensification).

The basic biocultural model shown in Figure 2.1 is intentionally generalized to incorporate and accommodate additional factors (i.e. mortuary context; historical documents) unique to the population, temporal-historical context, and particular problem researchers are attempting to explore. This model is not intended to capture a static or unidimensional progression of events, but rather to be used as a heuristic device that models and elucidates the multidimensional and dialectical relationship between the biological and cultural axes of lived experiences that leave evidence marked in human bodies (**individual, social, and political bodies**).

From a biocultural perspective, the observed variation within and between individuals and populations in terms of skeletal indicators of stress is understood to be a consequence of the phenotypic plasticity of the human body and skeleton. The concept of plasticity refers to the body's capability to elicit biological and behavioral responses that are dialectical with external stressors in the immediate environment (ecological, cultural, and social) (Zuckerman & Martin, 2016). These responses are observable at chemical, microscopic, and macroscopic levels, and because these biological responses are a product of the interaction between the body and its immediate environment, they are contextually contingent. Therefore, the body itself is contextually dependent (Sofaer, 2006: 74).

The concept of embodiment has been used to describe the relationship between the body (**individual, social, political**) and its environment (Zuckerman & Martin, 2016). Embodiment theory holds that humans incorporate the biological, physical, and social conditions of their immediate environment into their own biology. As such, this concept helps to explain how different patterns of disease, physiological stress, and trauma are found between different groups, because groups and the individuals they are comprised of are a product of their unique circumstances and experiences within their ecological, cultural, and social environments (Sofaer, 2006). However, humans are not inactive participants in this dynamic relationship, but active, both consciously and unconsciously, in shaping their own biology by their participation in the social world over their lifetime through intersecting and dynamic social identities (Agarwal, 2012: 137).

The biology of the human body changes as individuals grow and age over their lifespan. Life course theory has been used as a conceptual framework to explore the way age intersects with other biosocial aspects of the human condition, including sex and gender, to structure lived experiences of stress. As discussed previously life course theory contends that the skeleton represents an individual's accumulated lived experiences over their life course, which are determined by the biosocial reality in which that individual operated at any given stage of the life course (Agarwal, 2012: 142). Within this conceptual framework, at each stage of the life course, an individual is exposed to different stressors, and their ability to contend with those stressors (i.e. **Host Resistance Factors**) is determined by their experiences with similar or different stressors at earlier points in their development (Gowland, 2015).

Bioarchaeology's extensive engagement with the principles of plasticity, embodiment, and life-course imbues it with particularly salient frameworks for interrogating the relationships between the biosocial realities of social categories, identities, and social processes from skeletal past humans. When human remains are interpreted through these theoretical frameworks, it is possible to identify the social processes and mechanisms by which social and cultural constructs, such as gender, can become biological realities marked in bone.

The goals of investigating bioarchaeologies of gender are not to simply describe sex-based differences in the past, but to interrogate the intersection of individual biology with environmental contexts and social institutions to explore how social processes contribute to the production of differential experiences of disease, workload, trauma, and violence within and between groups. In bioarchaeology, the estimation of sex remains a fundamental step in the construction of the biological profile and is used to generate empirical data that can be used in comparative frameworks for interrogating observed patterns of pathology, activity, and trauma.

However, it is through the contextualization and theoretical interpretation of the observed patterns within and between biological categories such as sex and age and social categories such as status that afford bioarchaeologists the ability to say something about gender, gendered behaviors, and gendered experiences in the past (Knudson & Stojanowski, 2008). Bioarchaeology's engagement with gender theory over the last four decades has challenged researchers to not just document differential patterns of morbidity, mortality, and violence between men and women, but to interrogate other social categories such as age and status to capture observed patterns in more nuanced ways to interpret *how* and *why* the observed differences are socially meaningful within specific social, cultural, historical and temporal contexts (Zuckerman & Crandall, 2019).

Situating a Small-Scale Society in Time and Space: The Social and Political Climate in the AD 1100s

In order to understand the social meaning behind patterns of disease and trauma observable in the remains of the people who lived in these communities, we must consider the environmental and cultural stressors that these groups had to navigate. This is where the biocultural model of stress discussed above (Figure 2.1) is particularly useful for diagramming and thinking about types of stressors and

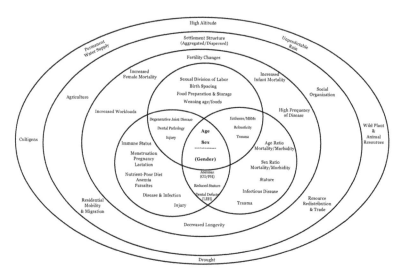

Figure 2.2 Biocultural model of stress for the La Plata River Valley communities.

how they intersect and interact with each other and with the body to construct individual lived experiences that are marked in the bones. The following discussion will situate the La Plata River Valley communities within their environmental, spatial, cultural, and temporal contexts and identify the potential sources of stress and their bodily manifestations. We have constructed a biocultural model for the La Plata River Valley as a visual representation of the context the individuals discussed in this volume navigated and the indicators of stress written on their bodies and in their bones (Figure 2.3).

Environment of the Northern San Juan Region

The La Plata River Valley is a high desert tributary of the San Juan River located in the northwest corner of modern-day New Mexico, close to the city of Farmington. The sites distributed along this river valley are concentrated in an area where the Animas, La Plata, and San Juan Rivers confluence to form a network of river valleys, called the *Tótah*, or "between the waters," by the Navajo (*Diné*) people who live there today (Martin & Osterholtz, 2016) (Figure 2.1).

Like much of the American Southwest, the Northern San Juan Region is characterized by environmental diversity, with significant topographic, climatic, and faunal variety occurring over short distances

(Kantner, 2004: 40). These differences, especially at the local level, contributed to a unique and diverse distribution of wild and domesticated plants and animals that supported and sustained local populations. The portion of the Colorado Plateau that includes the La Plata River Basin ranges in elevation between 6,000 and 8,500 feet, with the most arable lands suitable for dry-farming (the dominant agricultural strategy during pre-contact occupation of this region) located between 5,000 and 6,000 feet (Adams & Peterson, 1999: 19–26). The La Plata River Basin is situated between 5,000 and 6,800 feet above sea level but is permanently watered and consequently abundant with diverse natural resources (Potter & Chuipka, 2007) (Figure 2.4).

Temperatures within the Northern San Juan Region can range between 100 degrees Fahrenheit in the summer to −20 degrees Fahrenheit in the winter, with the average temperatures for the summer falling in the mid-80s. Most parts of this region experience just over 120 frost-free days, however at the higher elevations temperatures can suddenly drop below freezing as late as June and as early as September, resulting in crop-killing frosts (Adams & Peterson, 1999: 26). Precipitation in this region of the Southwest tends to fall most heavily in the higher elevations and reaches a maximum two times a year. This precipitation pattern is determined by large, shifting low-pressure systems driven by the Jet Stream, with maximum precipitation occurring between July and August, another peak from December through March, and a dry period between April and June (Cordell, 1997: 36).

In general, unpredictable rainfall, irregular water resources, and temperature extremes produced climatic and environmental diversity that resulted in variable distributions of agriculturally productive, or arable, soil, creating highly diverse agricultural landscapes across this region throughout its occupation. The variable distribution of arable land likely produced inequitable agricultural productivity between different locations occupied by groups throughout the region, which could have had implications for intergroup competition, conflict and raiding activities (Kantner, 2004: 40). However, regardless of the risk for crop failure due to the unpredictable rainfall and temperature variability macrobotanical, faunal, coprolite, and stable isotope analyses of bones suggest that maize was the most important food resource in this region by at least AD 600 (Varien et al., 2007) and comprised between 60% and 90% of the populations' diet (Kohler, 1992), with domesticated and wild animal species contributing marginally to their overall diet (Driver, 2002: 145) (Figure 2.5).

Likely due to its permanent water source, comparatively lush natural resources relative to neighboring regions, and consequentially

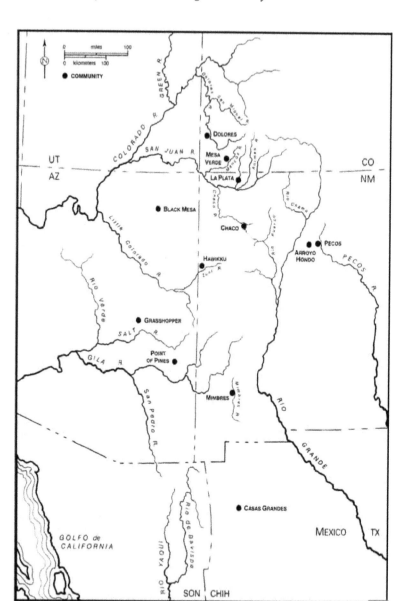

Figure 2.3 Map of the greater North American Southwest showing the location of the La Plata River Valley relative to other well-known archaeological sites in the region. Adapted from Martin et al. (2001).

Figure 2.4 Aerial view of the La Plata River along the New Mexico and Colorado borders. The Mesa Verde region is visible in the right background of this photo, highlighting the spatial proximity of the region to the La Plata River Valley. Note the topographic diversity of the region. Public Domain. Credit: Dicklyon, CC BY-SA 4.0, https://creativecommons.org/licenses/by-sa/4.0, via Wikimedia Commons. https://commons.wikimedia.org/wiki/File:La_Plata_River_aerial.jpg.

reliable domesticated and wild food resources, the La Plata River Valley was continuously occupied between AD 200 and 1300, with peak population density occurring between the 10th and 11th centuries AD, or the mid-Pueblo II (AD 900–1100) and early Pueblo III (AD 1100–1300) periods (Martin, 2008). Traditionally, a series of protracted drought conditions, collectively referred to as the "Great Drought," between AD 1276 and AD 1299 has been interpreted as the catalyst for the depopulation of the Northern San Juan region, including the La Plata River Valley. During this period, there was a marked reduction in annual precipitation, highly unpredictable seasonal precipitation patterns, a drop in the groundwater table, and loss of fertile soil deposits through floodplain erosion (Kantner, 2004: 43). The effects of this period of drought was likely exacerbated by the effects the Little Ice Age, which was a period of spatially extensive, cold and dry climatic conditions which Peterson (1988) suggested began to impact this region around AD 1200. During this period, winter precipitation decreased, the summer rains occurred later and didn't last as long, and the frost-free season shortened considerably, leaving very little time for crops to grow,

Figure 2.5 Rows of maize in a historic Hopi agricultural field plot near Tuba
City, Arizona 1941. Photographer: Ansel Adams (1902–1984), U.S.
National Archives and Records Administration, 1941. Public
Domain. Courtesy of the Department of the Interior, National
Park Service, branch of Still and Motion Pictures, via Wikimedia
Commons.

mature, and be harvested. Therefore, because the "Great Drought"
occurred during a period of population growth and aggregation into
large sites in the Northern San Juan region, it has been traditionally
argued that the prevailing agricultural strategy of the time, dry
farming, could not sustain the large populations within these environmental conditions (Peterson, 1988; Varien, 2010).

However, groups living in this region had successfully practiced high-
risk agriculture in a dynamic climatic and environmental context between at least AD 600 to AD 1275, and had weathered prolonged
droughts throughout their occupation, including one that occurred between AD 1130 and AD 1180 (Varien, 2010: 16), which impacted the La
Plata communities discussed in this volume. This suggests that these
groups had had cultural strategies designed to buffer these communities
against these environmental fluctuations that were successful, at least

until other factors came into play that precluded the effectiveness of these systems. Therefore, despite the comparatively resource-rich climate of the La Plata River Valley, these groups' reliance on maize agriculture in a high-altitude desert environment would have exposed them to increased risk for resource shortages. Agricultural resource shortages due to these environmental constraints, particularly during periods of increasing population density within a region, could be potentially disastrous for group morbidity (health) and mortality (death) when the cultural buffering systems against these constraints were unable to effectively protect the vulnerable members of these communities.

Cultural Systems and Cultural Stress

Cultural adaptations like agriculture, technology (e.g. food storage, processing, and cooking techniques), population aggregation, social organization and divisions of labor, and exchange networks provide a filter through which environmental constraints pass to safeguard groups against their negative effects. However, the marginal environment of the Northern San Juan region could produce severe enough stressors that could not be effectively mitigated, and cultural buffering systems could become additional sources of stress. Stress, as it is broadly used in this volume, refers to physiological disruptions in the body as a consequence of environmentally and culturally induced external insults (Goodman et al., 1988: 77).

As a consequence of the agricultural potential of the La Plata Valley, the region was able to sustain a substantial population throughout its occupation, which peaked during the PII (AD 900–1150) and PIII (AD 1150–1300) periods. Over the course of their occupation of the region, La Plata groups oscillated between living in dispersed and aggregated semi-permanent and permanent settlements composed of nuclear and extended households that formed dispersed communities interconnected through trading, networking, and shared ceremonial spaces (Dean & Van West, 2002: 152). The shifts in population size, density, and distribution through time had a significant impact on how sedentary and reliant on agriculture these groups were as well as the diseases they were at risk for experiencing.

Botanical and isotope analyses suggest increased reliance and steady intensification of maize agriculture over time in the La Plata River Valley (Martin et al., 2001; Toll, 1993). This increased reliance on maize through time, while advantageous in supporting the caloric requirements of a growing and densely concentrated population during ecologically favorable conditions for agriculture, could be problematic if there was crop failure several years in a row. This problem would be further compounded if group size was continuing to grow and if they invested in a rigid set of subsistence strategies (e.g. intensification of agriculture versus a mixed subsistence economy of agriculture and foraging). Furthermore, increasing reliance on maize relative to wild resources in a group's overall subsistence economy could have reduced the nutritional diversity of their diet, which could have implications for individuals' ability to obtain necessary nutrients for achieving their best health potentials (Martin et al., 2001). In this way a subsistence strategy emphasizing cultigens like maize can be both a buffer and a stressor depending on the environmental circumstances.

The PI (AD 750–900) and PIII (AD 1150–1350) periods in the La Plata River Valley were characterized by population growth and aggregation into fewer and more dispersed, but larger permanent settlements and settlement clusters (Figure 2.6). It has been suggested that this population aggregation was partly a behavioral adaptation to limited residential mobility as a consequence of the investment in increasing amounts of labor in agricultural food production, which necessitated

Figure 2.6 Taos Pueblo, New Mexico circa 1880, as an example of a multi-story adobe aggregated pueblo. Photographer: Cunningham & Co (1880–1889). Public Domain. Photo courtesy of the United States Library of Congress's Prints and Photographs Division http://hdl.loc.gov/loc.pnp/ppmsca.39909.

establishing permanent settlements (Varien et al., 1996: 102). Varien et al. (1996: 102) argue that the increased constraint on residential mobility forced groups to further invest in agricultural intensification. Agricultural intensification then led to increasing investment in settling in permanent locations. While this investment in agriculturally productive areas may have helped growing populations meet the caloric needs of the group, agricultural intensification also necessitated increased individual workloads and time investment in food processing (particularly for women). Furthermore, the aggregation of these groups into permanent settlements also exposed groups to an increased risk of exposure to communicable diseases and parasitic infections due to their crowded living conditions (Martin et al., 2001).

As population size and density increased through a combination of increased fertility and immigration within the context of unpredictable environmental conditions impacting crop yields, local exchange between communities likely became an increasingly important cultural strategy to buffer against environmental instability and resource shortages (Rautman, 1993). It has been argued that social networks are survival networks, conduits for information and resources to mitigate the effects of local resource unpredictability, and pathways along which groups can migrate (Borck et al., 2015). Following this logic, the types of social networks utilized by different groups in the American Southwest may have differentially impacted their abilities to cope with external stressors.

The communities living along the La Plata River Valley were situated between and contemporaneous with the socio-political and economic hubs centered within the Mesa Verde region to the north and Chaco Canyon to the south, embedding them within rich and dynamic socio-political, economic, and ideological interaction spheres. Therefore, the communities in the La Plata River Valley may have also developed and maintained integrated social networks between the dispersed and aggregated communities within and outside the region through which food and other resources like people, material goods, and information could be moved and redistributed in times of environmentally induced stress. As a result of this proximity, the La Plata communities were likely impacted by the activities, social changes, and economic opportunities taking place in the neighboring regions (Martin et al., 2001). Furthermore, because of the proximity of the La Plata communities to these regional socio-political hubs, these communities likely also experienced comparatively high population density and its associated negative health consequences from communicable diseases while also contending with the effects of resource stress during ecologically unfavorable conditions for agricultural production (Martin et al., 2001).

Toward the end of the PII period (AD 900–1150), and of particular importance to understanding the situation for the women at La Plata discussed in this volume, population growth within the region slowed significantly, with some individuals emigrating out of the La Plata Valley, potentially headed for the communities living at Chaco Canyon and Mesa Verde (Cordell & McBrinn, 2016: 197, 208). These end-of-PII changes were concurrent with a protracted period of drought that impacted the entire region and lasted for approximately 50 years (AD 1130–1180). Varien et al. (1996: 102) suggest that the prolonged deterioration of environmental conditions and population decline during the late PII and early PIII periods were also accompanied by less trading and collaboration as well as decreased residential mobility between the communities within the La Plata River Valley, and the Northern San Juan region in general. This would have forced communities to increase the amount of produce from their fields by intensifying their agricultural efforts. This intensification is evidenced by the increase in the number of field houses near the crops, terracing of the fields, dams on the river, irrigation troughs, and artificial reservoirs. These changes to the local environment to enhance the landscape for farming also meant people were more invested and tied to one place, further decreasing their options for residential mobility. Some archaeologists have noted that the aggregation of communities around defensible resources like land and water set in motion more rigid social systems (e.g. social hierarchies, gender roles) than what had been in effect previously. Therefore, during the time period when the La Plata women were living, there was an interruption of farming and the political-economic social structures which previously facilitated redistribution and sharing of resources were being replaced by more rigid social boundaries that revolved around the increased need to protect access to arable land and reliable water sources.

A breakdown in the subsistence and sociopolitical systems facilitating resource redistribution in the context of environmental uncertainty and increasing population pressure may have also increased competition-induced conflict. In some circumstances the La Plata River Valley communities may have opted to invest in stratified social arrangements to control the means of production and redistribution during times of resource and/or population-induced stress, with some members retaining unequal access to food and other productive resources. As a result, subgroups within these communities would be put at higher risk for greater workloads, disease, and early death compared to others, which could result in interpersonal conflict between competing and/or oppressed members of the group. Evidence used to argue for increased interpersonal conflict during the late PII and PIII periods include the aggregation of communities within canyon systems and the increased construction of "defensive" architecture, including cliff-dwellings, fortified walls, and multi-storied towers constructed around settlements with access to water resources within canyon settings (Haas & Creamer, 1996; Leblanc, 1999) (Figure 2.7). There is also a diverse range of skeletal evidence for violent conflict throughout the Puebloan populations occupying the neighboring Mesa Verde and Chaco Canyon regions during this time period (Harrod, 2013; Kuckelman, 2012; Osterholtz, 2018). This suggests that conflict was likely a common feature of life in the Northern San Juan region; however, the general consensus within the literature is that raiding for resources and captives was the more common form of conflict than actual warfare (Kuckelman, 2012).

Thus, it wasn't just climate change or environmental degradation that pushed these farming communities out of their river valleys; there was likely also a looming sense of anxiety and threat of increased conflict in the form of raiding for women and other captives and diminishing the competition for scarce resources (LeBlanc, 1999: 153). It seems probable that, collectively, all of these issues created synergistic and contextually contingent factors that would have pressed in on both men's and women's daily lives in important ways. As resources depleted due to prolonged drought, exploitation of the local resources, and increasing population density, competition between communities who were formally allies and workmates may have intensified into conflicts, raiding, and retaliation.

Individual Physiology

Not all individuals in a population are equally at risk for experiencing stress. The impact of stress on an individual will vary depending on a number of factors, including the individual's age, sex, overall health, and immune system status. Healthy individuals will usually be able to resist severe stressors in most circumstances and survive. However, individuals who are already immunologically, metabolically, and nutritionally compromised due to natural, pathological, or cultural processes may not be able to resist or recover from even mild stressors.

Ecological and cultural stresses tend to have the most significant impact on individuals with immature or compromised immune systems, such as infants, weanlings, pregnant and lactating women, the

Figure 2.7 "Hopi girls outside an adobe cliff-dwelling circa 1906." Note the limited accessibility of the dwelling location. Photographer: Edward S. Curtis (1868–1952). Public Domain. Photo courtesy of the United States Library of Congress's Prints and Photographs Division. http://hdl.loc.gov/loc.pnp/cph.3c12228.

elderly, and the infirmed who are already physiologically compromised due to disease or injury (Larsen, 2015). During periods of resource shortages, inadequate access to nutrition combined with exposure to high pathogen loads (e.g. aggregated settlement living conditions) and/ or chronic physical abuse can negatively impact the health of individuals who are already at risk for poor health and make them more susceptible to disease and/or early death.

An individual's physiology is simultaneously a biological and cultural state because cultural factors, like gender and socioeconomic status and the resources available to an individual based on those factors, can protect or predispose biologically vulnerable individuals to morbidity or early mortality. As an example, Perry (2004) correlated indicators of muscularity and use of the body with evidence of nutritional stress and isotopic analyses to show that a rigid, sex-based division of labor existed at Grasshopper Pueblo (AD 1275–1400) and that it resulted in disproportionately poorer health for women relative to men. She argues that the social, spatial, and ideological constraints imposed by the sexually structured division of labor organizing the community (e.g. a cultural system) precluded women from accessing protein-rich resources such as meat, resulting in an increased risk for dietary stress.

The effects of stress not only impact the physical well-being of those experiencing it but can have lasting implications throughout an individual's development and adulthood, as well as have enduring effects that carry over into their children and subsequent descendent generations (Gravlee, 2009; Shonkoff et al., 2012). When adults are disproportionately exposed to increased risk for poor health or violence, through poverty or a disadvantaged social status, their children are also exposed and affected. Exposure to stressors during childhood development, including while in *utero*, has lasting implications for adult health (see Aiken & Ozanne, 2013; Barker, 1997). This becomes a self-sustaining cycle of inequality, which promotes the status quo that set the cycle in motion and creates a subgroup of disproportionately poor and sickly individuals, without access to the resources to improve their social, economic, or biological (health) status (Gravlee, 2009).

Skeletal Indicators of Stress

When individuals are unable to resist stress, physiological disruption occurs. The type and severity of physiological disruption are dependent on the individual's physiology, and whether the stressors are acute (e.g. injury) or chronic (e.g. malnutrition, parasitic infection). If stress is severe and protracted enough, it will manifest skeletally in identifiable and interpretable ways. Therefore, skeletal markers of stress can be used to reconstruct the demographic and biological impact of lived experiences of morbidity during infancy, childhood, and adult life.

Skeletal indicators of growth disruption, disease and death are usually produced by prolonged or repeated exposure to physiological stress (Ortner, 2003). While bone tissue responds to stress in nonspecific and generalized ways, the type, frequency, severity, and distribution of these markers on the body and along age and sex categories can provide insight into what biological systems may have been involved. When interpreted within their ecological and cultural context, these markers can be suggestive of the types of environmental and cultural stress (e.g. disease, violence) that may have produced them and the comparative success or failure of cultural systems to buffer vulnerable subgroups against them.

There are numerous stress indicators that manifest on the bones and teeth which are used in bioarchaeological analyses to draw inferences about the presence and nature of stress and its functional and adaptive (or maladaptive) effects on individuals and groups. For instance, because the body's immune response to pathogens is energetically costly, it can result in trade-offs with physical growth and development in children (Garcia et al., 2020; Urlacher et al., 2018: E3914). This understanding is well established in bioarchaeology, where researchers have long used childhood stature, achieved adult stature, and physiological markers of arrested growth such as Harris Lines and dental defects like linear enamel hypoplasias (Figure 2.8) as markers of childhood nutritional and disease stress because they not only manifest in the bones of infants and children but persist into adulthood and provide a temporally sensitive record (memory) of survived childhood stress (Larsen, 2015). Other dental pathologies, such as dental attrition (wear), caries (cavities), abscesses, and antemortem tooth-loss (Figure 2.9) can provide general information on the nature of the diet (e.g. carbohydrate heavy) and oral health in adults, particularly when combined with other skeletal indicators of nutritional stress and archaeological reconstructions.

Porosities of the skull (porotic hyperostosis [PH]) (Figure 2.10) and on the roofs of the orbits (cribra orbitalia [CO]) (Figure 2.11) are the most ubiquitous skeletal indicators of stress observed in ancestral Indigenous a American Southwest groups and are generally believed to be caused by acquired, dietary and/or genetic anemias (Walker et al., 2009, Oxenham & Cavill, 2010). Traditionally, these lesions are associated with conditions like lack of iron and vitamin B_{12} in the diet,

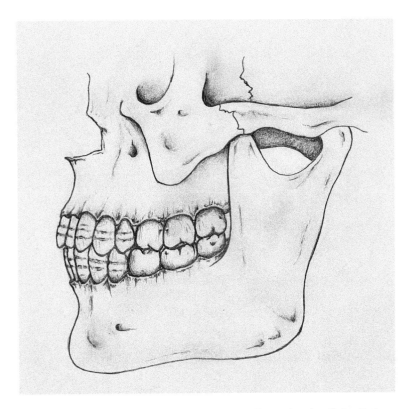

Figure 2.8 Linear enamel hypoplasias (LEH). Illustration by Claira Ralston.

breastfeeding activities, diarrheal disease, parasitic infections, and dense, unsanitary living conditions, all of which contribute to generalized anemia disorders. Several studies have argued for separate but related underlying diseases that can lead to the development of PH and CO lesions . For instance, recent studies by Rivera & Mirazón Lahr (2017), Cole & Waldron (2019) and O'Donnell (2019) provide convincing evidence that PH and CO may be produced by different underlying conditions. For example, PH, which is associated with marrow expansion in cranial bones, is suggested to be caused by nutritional stress (iron deficiency, Vitamin B_{12} deficiency) and infectious disease. CO is proposed to have a more complicated etiology, where its co-occurrence with marrow expansion/PH suggests it is caused by a similar disease process as PH. However, when CO is not associated with marrow expansion, it is thought to be more likely the result of anemia due to chronic disease

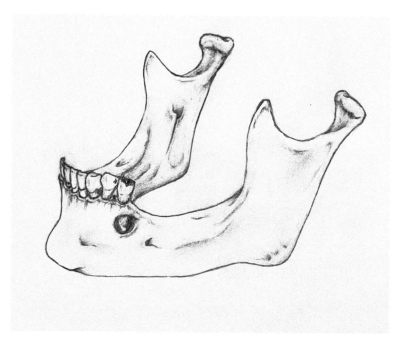

Figure 2.9 Dental abscess and antemortem tooth loss. Illustration by Claira
Ralston.

or scurvy (Rivera & Mirazón Lahr, 2017). The presence, prevalence, and
severity of these lesions across age and sex categories provide information on the experiences of physiological stress as it relates to food
resource allocation and exposure to disease between individuals and
subgroups at La Plata.

Periosteal reactions (i.e. periostitis) (Figure 2.12) are bony lesions that
are frequently interpreted to be produced by the body's generalized
inflammatory reaction on the periosteum of bone in response to prolonged or chronic (bacterial) infections and trauma (Buikstra, 2019).
These lesions are variously described as raised, longitudinally striated
and spiculated patches of porous/woven-looking immature bone and
plaque-like deposits of remodeling new bone formation, depending on
whether the lesions were active or healing at the time of the affected
individual's death (Buikstra, 2019; Rothschild & Jellema, 2020). These
lesions are generally regarded as a nonspecific indicator of systemic infectious disease because a large number of pathological conditions can
produce periosteal reactions, so the differential diagnosis of the exact

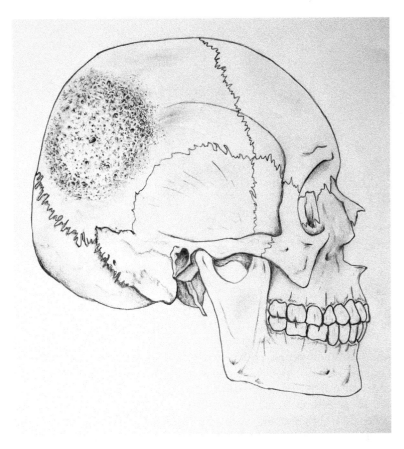

Figure 2.10 Porotic hyperostosis (PH). Illustration by Claira Ralston.

disease or pathogen producing them is difficult (Roberts & Buikstra, 2019). Generally speaking, these lesions have traditionally been associated with infections by *Staphylococcus aureus* or other forms of *Streptococcus* bacteria (Roberts & Brickley, 2018). Furthermore, there are some specific bacterial diseases that have differentially diagnostic manifestations, distributions, and patterns of periosteal lesions on skeletal remains, including osteomyelitis, tuberculosis, brucellosis, pneumonia, leprosy, treponematosis (yaws, venereal syphilis), cholera, and plague (Buikstra, 2019). The presence, location, severity (extent of involvement), and stage of healing of these lesions and their distribution along age and sex categories are important for identifying other types of

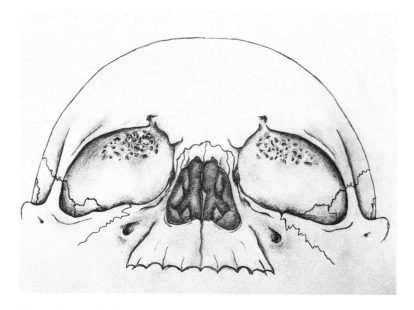

Figure 2.11   Cribria orbitalia (CO). Illustration by Claira Ralston.

disease stress impacting past groups (morbidity burden), particularly subgroups within a population, and what they can reveal about the broader environment (e.g. crowded, unsanitary) past peoples negotiated.

Other skeletal markers of stress, such as bone robusticity (thickness and density), entheses, and osteoarthritis reflect the amount of activity and labor an individual participated in during life. Entheses, also known as musculo-skeletal stress markers (MSMs), are roughened and raised sites where muscles, ligaments, and tendons originate or insert onto and into bones and develop in proportion to the amount of use those muscles get (Figures 2.13–2.15). Their degree of development (low-medium, high, very high) are useful indicators of the excessive use of particular muscles or joint complexes (e.g. elbow, shoulder, hip, knee). Osteoarthritis (OA) is a chronic degenerative joint disorder caused primarily by prolonged biomechanical wear and tear at joint surfaces, including all vertebral and appendage joint systems, but it can also result from traumatic injuries near or associated with joints (Figures 2.16–2.18). Measurements of robusticity, enthesial development, and OA are useful indicators of excessive activity patterns that can be used to detect disproportionate experiences of more or less activity among subgroups within a population.

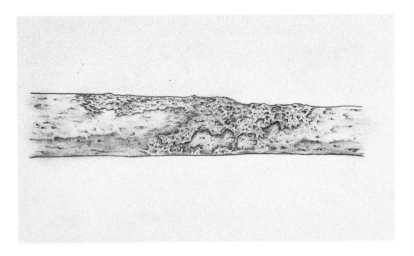

Figure 2.12 Periosteal reaction on a long bone shaft. Illustration by Claira Ralston.

Trauma is another particularly useful and easily identifiable marker of stress. The type (e.g. cranial or postcranial), timing (e.g. healed, healing, not healed), severity, size, and distribution of traumatic injuries to the skeleton can reflect occupation-related or violence-related injuries depending on the context wherein they were received (Figure 2.19). Occupation-related or violence-related injuries reflect different types and mechanisms producing stress, but neither is less significant for understanding the impact of these injuries on an individual's ability to survive and the social systems that either predisposed them to, or protected them from, getting injured and supporting them after they were injured. The distribution of different types and timing of traumatic injuries along sex and age lines can be particularly illustrative of cultural systems that disproportionately expose certain subgroups to more or less risk for injury and the social and/or ideological purposes or significance of the behaviors that produced those injuries (e.g. Harrod, 2012; Martin, 2008; Osterholtz, 2014).

Impact of Stress on the Population

The skeletal indicators of physiological stress discussed above provide information on the types and impacts of stress on past populations, which feeds directly back into understanding the role that individual

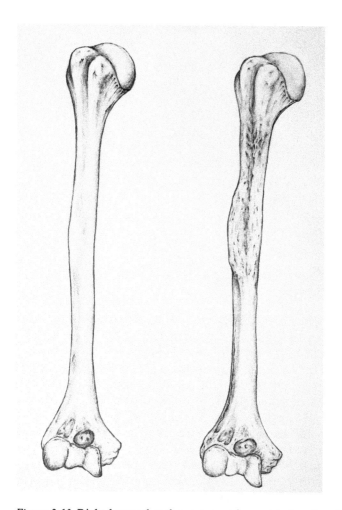

Figure 2.13 Right humeral entheses comparison, anterior view. The illustration on the left demonstrates low development of the pectoralis
major, deltoideus, and brachioradialis muscle attachments; the
illustration on the right demonstrates high development and
rugosity of the same muscle attachments. Illustrations by Claira
Ralston.

biology, cultural systems, and the environment collectively play in
promoting or preventing experiences of poor health, injury, and death.
The relationships between all of these interacting factors intersect and
interact in different ways depending on the context to produce variable

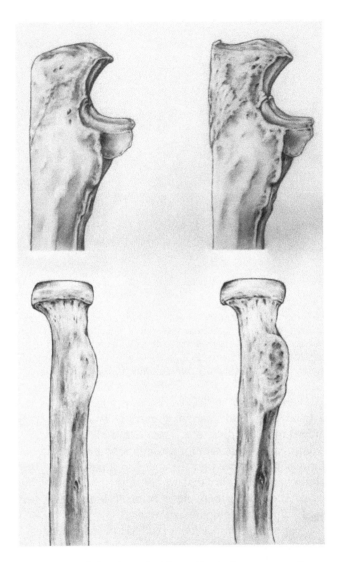

Figure 2.14 Right ula and right radius entheses comparison, anterior-lateral view. The upper left illustration demonstrates low development of the triceps brachii muscle attachment of the proximal ulna; the upper right demonstrates high development and rugosity of the same muscle attachment. The lower left illustration demonstrates low development of the biceps-brachii muscle attachment of the proximal radius; the lower right demonstrates high development and rugosity of the same muscle attachment. Illustrations by Claira Ralston.

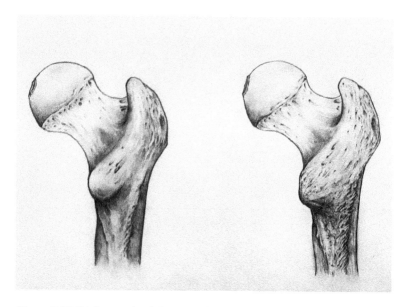

Figure 2.15 Right proximal femur entheses comparison, posterior view. The illustration on the left demonstrates low development of the gluteus maximus and iliopsoas muscle attachments; the illustration on the right demonstrates high development and rugosity of the same muscle attachments. Illustrations by Claira Ralston.

individual, social, and political bodies, which is why we chose to visually represent them in a Venn diagram Figures (2.1 and 2.2). It is important to understand how disease and death can have significant functional and adaptive consequences for a community because it is in these causal relationships that we find the social meaning behind the patterns of morbidity and mortality that we see in the bones and why some subgroups of individuals may have been at higher risk for morbidity and early mortality compared to others.

While physiological disruption occurs at the level of the individual, it can have implications for overall health and survival at household and community levels. Severe and prolonged malnutrition among members of a community can negatively impact their capacity for work, fertility, and mortality; which can disrupt and destabilize the social, economic, and political systems of support, causing further stress. For instance, while poor health occasionally results in death, it also decreases the work capacity of individuals for acquiring and preparing necessary resources to meet the increasing demands of a

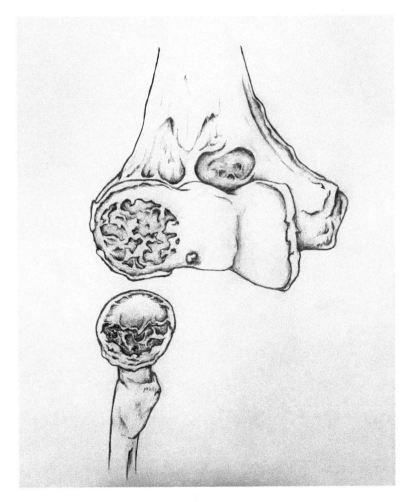

Figure 2.16 Osteoarthritis (OA) of the distal right humerus and corresponding arthritic changes to the proximal right radius. Illustrations by Claira Ralston.

growing population, which can result in further resource stress. High morbidity and mortality in young adult women and pregnant or lactating women can impact the reproductive capacity of a group, resulting in higher infant mortality, the overall loss of population, and consequently loss of productive capacity for meeting subsistence needs (Martin et al., 1991). Furthermore, debilitating or chronic health

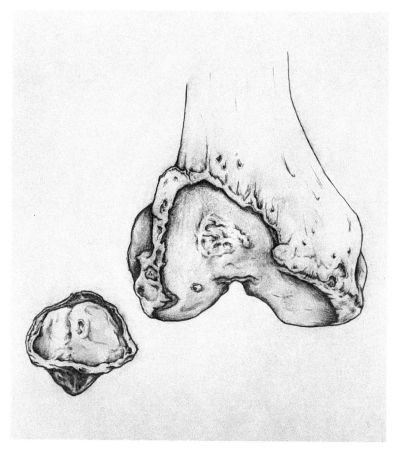

Figure 2.17 Osteoarthritis (OA) of the distal right femur (anterior view) and corresponding arthritic changes to the right patella (posterior view). Illustrations by Claira Ralston.

problems can also disrupt the patterning of reciprocal social interactions and social unity and consequently strain the social systems of support.

La Plata: Cultural Diseases, Social Bodies

The study of skeletonized bodies is challenging, but there has been a fluorescence in new techniques to "read" the body for signs of use and disuse, health and disease, and violence and trauma (see Mann &

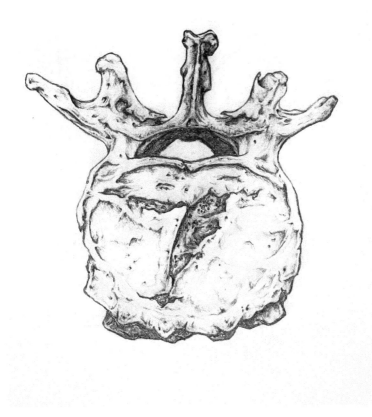

Figure 2.18 Osteoarthritis (OA) in a lumbar vertebra, superior view. Note the osteophytic lipping along the anterior margin of the vertebral body and transverse processes, and the Schmorl's node in the center of the vertebral body. Illustrations by Claira Ralston.

Hunt, 2013 for a full photographic listing of pathological alterations that can be seen on bones). While there are many health problems that do not leave signatures on the skeletal system or kill individuals so quickly that skeletal lesions do not have time to develop (i.e. acute conditions), there are also many common and highly prevalent pathogens that cause illness and do initiate changes in bone tissue over time (i.e. chronic conditions). These include numerous conditions that produce various anemias (e.g. nutritional deficiencies, thalassemia, malaria, etc.), bacterial infections (e.g. staphylococcus, streptococcus,

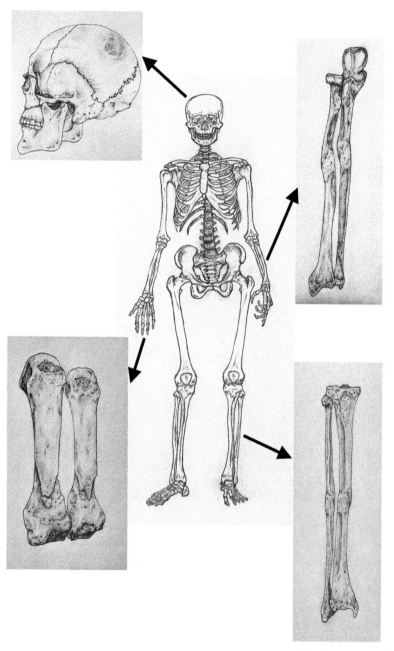

(caption on next page)

treponemas), respiratory ailments (i.e. tuberculosis), gastrointestinal problems (e.g. parasitic or bacterial infection). These are precisely the conditions that people today living in marginalized and underserved settings die from in high frequencies (https://www.healthypeople.gov/ 2020/topics-objectives/topic/social-determinants-health/interventions-resources/poverty).

As discussed and illustrated above in Figures 2.1 and 2.2, patterns of death and disease are not random occurrences. They are intimately linked to every facet of lifestyle from diet and climate to occupation, social structure, and religion. Pathological conditions found within the La Plata population are briefly summarized here to frame the types of physiological trials the men, women, and children of La Plata faced as they went about their daily tasks within the environmental, social, and political climate of AD 1100. This information is drawn from the summary volume published by Martin and colleagues (2001), which the reader is encouraged to download for free (http://www.nmarchaeology. org/assets/files/archnotes/242.pdf) for a more in-depth reporting of the methods and data used in the analyses of these individual burials. What follows below is an abbreviated summary.

The La Plata individuals discussed in this volume are represented by a total of 67 individuals and is comprised of 30 non-adults and 37 adults (19 females, 16 males, and 3 undetermined). Using standardized osteological data collection methods (see Martin et al., 2001), data on age at death, sex, stature, pathology, musculo-skeletal indicators of physical activity (e.g. robusticity and enthesal development), and trauma from all individual burials were collected. These data were evaluated in combination with mortuary and archaeological contexts to explore whether subgroups with disparate experiences of health, workloads, and trauma could be detected, as well as compared to patterns in other populations throughout the American Southwest. The pathological indicators analyzed by Martin and colleagues (2001) include porotic hyperostosis, subadult and adult stature, linear enamel hypoplasias, dental pathologies (dental attrition/wear, caries, ante-mortem tooth loss), nonspecific infections in the form of periosteal reactions, degenerative diseases of joints (osteoarthritis), and trauma (discussed in Chapter 3). These skeletal indicators of stress were

Figure 2.19 Examples of antemortem fractures typically observed on different parts of the body, including the cranium, radius and ulna (forearm), tibia and fibula (leg), and metacarpals (bones of the palm). All elements are from the right side. Illustrations by Claira Ralston.

selected for analysis by Martin and colleagues (2001) because they provided conspicuous information on demography and disease and allowed for comparative analyses by future researchers.

In general, nutritional stress, as expressed by porotic hyperostosis lesions, and its associated health complications were ubiquitous among the La Plata individuals, but not a source of severe health issues. About half of the infants and children analyzed showed signs of nutritional stress in the form of porotic hyperostosis at the time of their deaths; however, none of the children exhibited severe expressions and nearly all of the cases were healing at the time these individuals died. This suggests that infants in children were exposed to low-level, but persistent nutritional stresses, likely from weaning and seasonal food resource stress. This interpretation is supported by the low frequency and numbers of linear enamel hypoplasias (LEH) in the subadult and adult permanent dentition. These LEH lesions tended to develop when the individuals were between 1.5 and 5 years of age, which according to ethnographic and ethnohistoric records was around the age where infants were weaned among Puebloan groups (Babcock, 1991; Hill, 1982). Weaning is a particularly physiologically stressful period for infants and young children, driven by the lower nutritional quality of postweaning foods and an increased susceptibility to infectious diseases as a result of a weaker immune system during this pivotal period of development.

Nutritional inadequacies were also found to be an equal burden for adult men and women (about a third each exhibited porotic hyperostosis lesions consistent with nutritional deficiencies), suggesting that both consumed similar diets and shared similar risks for experiencing dietary stressors. When compared to other farming communities in the broader American Southwest region, the rates of porotic hyperostosis exhibited between the children and adult individuals in the La Plata burial population are among the lowest (Martin et al., 2001: 66). Furthermore, when examining the overall achieved stature of adults and the growth and development of children in terms of their long bone lengths at the time of death, the La Plata children and adults fall well within a normal distribution when compared with past groups living in the desert environments of the American Southwest. Collectively, these data suggest that the farming potential of the La Plata Valley was generally better than the landscapes accessible to the communities farther away from perennial water sources and that the La Plata communities did not experience severe resource shortages for extended periods of time.

There is a synergistic relationship between nutritional inadequacies and susceptibility to transmissible infectious diseases. At La Plata, nutritional inadequacies in children and women tended to co-occur with common transmissible infections. Of the children showing nutritional problems, about half also had skeletal lesions consistent with non-specific infectious disease (manifested as periosteal reactions). Roberts and Brickley (2018) show that infectious diseases find more "willing" hosts in malnourished or anemic individuals. Of the adult population, while men and women equally exhibited porotic hyperostosis lesions, adult women exhibited five times more lesions consistent with non-specific infections, suggesting that adult women were exposed to a greater risk than men for infectious disease. The presence of nutritional problems and infections among the La Plata burial population is comparable to the 2018 State of Health in New Mexico report (New Mexico Department of Health, 2018: 64), where it was found that the highest cause of death in Native American groups is influenza and pneumonia. One child (approximately nine years of age) from La Plata (LA 37599 B6) exhibited periosteal reactions and fusion between vertebral bodies that were consistent with tuberculosis, a chronic infectious disease. Tuberculosis, like all communicable diseases, is often associated with communities of individuals who live together in close proximity and are experiencing lowered immune resistance and function and has significant time depth in the Americas (Gómez i Prat Mendonça de Souza, 2003). Another individual, a 25-year-old woman (LA 37601, B4) exhibited macroscopic and radiologic lesions consistent with osteomyelitis, which is a severe bacterial infection that has worked its way into the bone marrow, either by a direct introduction from trauma, from skin infections that spread to the bone, and/or by other vascular routes into the bone that are connected to the original site of infection (Buikstra, 2019; Ortner, 2003). This suggests that the La Plata communities were also at risk for infection by a range of communicable diseases, likely as a consequence of the more crowded living conditions of aggregated settlement arrangements.

Older adults at La Plata suffered with degenerative joint diseases like OA just like older adults do today. About half of the adults (both men and women) showed some wear-and-tear on their joint systems. All of the cases for individuals 50 years or younger exhibited mild to moderate expressions of bony degenerative changes consistent with OA. The two oldest men (50+) at La Plata presented with more moderate to severe expressions of OA, which we can imagine may have resulted in complaints about their "aching backs." That being said, we must be cautious about correlating bony changes with pain, as pain can also be present in the absence of bony changes. What the presence of these bony changes among these individuals reflect is an accumulation of stress and strain from the habitual use of their musculoskeletal systems that may or may not have affected their mobility and quality of life later in life. The presence of OA among the older individuals within the La Plata burial population is not unusual for past and historic populations in the American Southwest and is consistent with robusticity and entheses data suggesting that individuals within the La Plata communities undertook heavy workloads throughout most of their lifespan.

Finally, one young adult woman (age 18 to 20) (LA 37601 B2) is notable among the La Plata burial population because of an extensive series of osteolytic (bone destroying) lesions on most of the bones of the upper body, pelvis, and hips. Based on the macroscopic and radiographic characteristics and distributions of the osteolytic lesions throughout this individual's body, Martin and colleagues (2001) found that this young adult woman may have had a metastatic carcinoma. The morphology and patterning of the osteolytic lesions fits the descriptive characteristics of metastatic carcinoma. Furthermore, their distribution throughout this woman's body is consistent with how this disease affects skeletal tissues, where cancer cells travel and infect skeletal tissues throughout the body from the primary site of a tumor through the vascular and marrow passages that permeate our bones (Ortner & Putschar, 1981: 392). The concentrations, severity, and distribution of these osteolytic lesions could also be suggestive of a potential primary tumor site. For this individual, the lesions appear to have affected the pelvic area more severely than the rest of the bones, followed by the spine and ribs, with a few of the lesions in these areas exhibiting some remodeling. This suggests that the primary tumor may have originated somewhere in the gastrointestinal or renal areas before spreading elsewhere throughout the body. Cancers are comparatively rare in the archaeological record, although they are not absent. This is because individuals with untreated metastatic carcinomas typically die fairly early in the course of the disease, which leaves little time for cancer to affect the bones. In the case of this young woman, she likely lived with the disease for a prolonged period of time before it either killed her, or she succumbed to a secondary infection from one of the communicable diseases affecting the population as a consequence of her weakened immune system.

The inventory of diseases at La Plata is not extensive, but it is important in that it represents the common everyday challenges experienced by women, men, and children in Southwest desert farming groups. The La Plata communities suffered from a typical range of ailments for these populations, including nutritional issues, infectious diseases, and heavy workloads. There was no rampant starvation nor were there individuals who carried a morbidity burden that was out of the ordinary for the region and time period. The general physiological involvement among the La Plata individuals is slight to moderate for nutritional problems and infection, and when compared with other Southwest groups, shows that they were on the low end of the frequency distribution. Oral pathologies (attrition/wear, caries, antemortem tooth loss, abscesses) at La Plata likewise fall well within the low end of the frequencies for contemporaneous Southwest groups. The occurrence of tuberculosis in one of the subadult burials is not unusual; there have been many reported cases in pre-contact North American Southwest skeletal populations (i Prat & Mendonça de Souza, 2003). The single case of probable metastatic cancer is somewhat unique and may be among the first documented for the American Southwest in a young woman. Therefore, the bones tell a story of mild to moderate daily physiological disruptions that may have contributed to morbidity, but not necessarily to large-scale mortality among the La Plata communities.

Gender Roles and Implications for Inequities

Researchers have suggested that aggregation and the social strategies intended to integrate the different households and kin groups that came with it during the PI and early PIII periods had significant implications for the assignment and formalization of labor tasks and differential access to social power and experiences of physiological stress (Roth, 2010a; Perry, 2004). While the shift to aggregated communities generally resulted in an emphasis on communal labor, many archaeological studies suggest that labor tasks also became more differentiated along sex and gender lines as a result of agricultural intensification, craft specialization, and community integration strategies, especially those associated with ritual feasting activities (Crown, 2000; Perry & Joyce, 2001). This is evidenced by the increasingly segregated spatial organization of material processing and production areas within the village and the distribution of tools associated with ethnographically and ethnohistorically gendered tasks in burials from the post AD 1150 period across the American Southwest (Mills, 2000; Perry, 2004; Roth, 2010b).

It is likely that social practices may have been driving these patterns. Specifically, the performance of everyday gendered tasks in formalized ritual enactments and contexts contributes to the socialization for and regulation of gendered roles (Perry & Joyce, 2001: 66). The process of formalizing gendered tasks through ritual performance naturalizes the association of specific persons with particular roles and tasks. It also regulates those individuals' behaviors through the ritual performance of those tasks wherein the public evaluation of an individuals' conformity to idealized expectations can occur (Perry & Joyce, 2001: 66). In this way, increasingly rigid sex-based and gendered divisions of labor can become socially sanctioned and embedded into the mechanisms of social power.

For example, Perry (2004) correlated measures of robusticity and entheses development with evidence of nutritional stress to show that a rigid, sex-based division of labor existed at Grasshopper Pueblo (AD 1275–1400) and that it resulted in disproportionately poorer health for adult women relative to men. She argues that the social, spatial, and ideological constraints imposed by the sexually structured division of labor organizing the community precluded women from accessing protein-rich resources like meat, resulting in dietary stress. Therefore, as Perry (2004) demonstrated, increasingly rigid divisions of labor and restriction of individuals to specific activities have the potential to produce disproportionate experiences of poor health between men and women, as well as between females and between men.

Perry's (2004) analyses are complemented by a recent study by Reynolds et al. (2020), which examined the relationship between gender norms in the matrilineally and patrilineally organized subpopulations of the Mosuo of China and health disparities (measured by chronic inflammation and hypertension) between men and women within these different sociocultural institutions. Reynolds and colleagues (2020) found that among the matrilineally organized Mosuo groups, which favor gender norms promoting women's autonomy and access to resources, men and women exhibited relatively equitable experiences of good health and disease. Conversely, they found that women in the patrilineally organized Mosuo groups, which favor gender norms biased toward men's social power, women disproportionately exhibited poorer health outcomes and chronic disease experiences than men. These authors suggest that, among the Mosuo, gender norms in matriliny organized social groups have a protective effect on women and an insignificant effect on men. Reynolds and colleagues (2020) concluded that, because women's experiences of poor health change drastically between matrilineally and patrilineally organized groups of the same population while men's stay relatively the same, social (e.g. gender) institutions do have measurable biological consequences for men and women that contribute to gendered disparities in experiences of health and disease. Therefore, Perry's (2004) bioarchaeological analyses of sexual divisions of labor and health and Reynolds et al.'s (2020) study of the relationship between health and gendered social institutions illustrate the intimate relationship between gendered disparities in health and disease and socio-cultural institutions that promote inequitable access to resources and social power between men and women.

Summary

To understand the lived experiences of individuals in the distant past we must first place them back into the world they navigated. This chapter was a dive into what is currently known about the archaeologically and ethnographically reconstructed environment and cultural systems of the communities living in La Plata River Valley throughout the AD 1000s. Using the biocultural model of stress, we situated the La Plata communities within their environmental, spatial, cultural, and temporal contexts to provide a framework through which we identified potential sources of stress and their manifestations in the bodies of individuals.

The picture that emerges for the La Plata communities is one of an agricultural population that faced common everyday challenges experienced by women, men, and children in many desert farming groups. They suffered from a typical range of ailments for populations subscribing to agrarian lifeways, including nutritional issues, infectious diseases, and heavy workloads. Despite the crowded living conditions and exposure to infectious disease, subsistence risks in a marginal desert environment, and nutritional deficits that tend to accompany dependence on agriculture, the La Plata communities were doing comparatively well in terms of morbidity and mortality relative to their neighbors. Generally speaking, life was pretty good for the communities living at La Plata. However, all of this is shadowed by the high frequencies of trauma found in a small cohort of women within the larger population. The high frequencies of cranial trauma, combined with evidence of disproportionately excessive workloads and careless mortuary treatments are evocative of an undercurrent of pain and suffering for a small, but significant group.

We closed this chapter with a brief discussion of gender roles and their implications for inequities in access to social power and their consequential role in structuring differential experiences of health, disease, and trauma between men and women. Perry's (2004) bioarchaeological analysis and Reynolds et al.'s (2020) medical anthropological study, while using different approaches and taking place at different points in time, are significant in that they all locate the embeddedness of gendered disparities in social institutions and relations of power. This relationship not only structures inequities in experiences of poor health and trauma between men and women within social arrangements, but also between women and between men. This is particularly evident in the experiences of the small group of women who appeared to have been disproportionately beaten and worked to the bone compared to their age-matched counterparts, suggesting an undercurrent of targeted gender violence at La Plata that is discussed in the following chapter.

References

Adams, K.R., & Peterson, K.L. (1999) Environment. In W.D. Lipe, M.D. Varien, and R.H. Wilshusen (Eds.), *Colorado prehistory: A context for the Southern Colorado river basin* (pp. 14–49). Colorado Council of Professional Archaeologists.

Agarwal, S.C. (2012) The past of sex, gender, and health: Bioarchaeology of the aging skeleton. *American Anthropologist* 114(2), 322–335. DOI:10.1111/j.1548-1433.2012.01428.x.

Aiken, C.E., & Ozanne, S.E. (2013). Sex differences in developmental programming models. *Reproduction*, 145(1), R1–R13.

Babcock, B.A. (Ed.) (1991). *Pueblo mothers and children: Essays by elsie clews parsons 1915–1924*. Ancient City Press.

Barker, D.J. (1997). Maternal nutrition, fetal nutrition, and disease in later life. *Nutrition*, 13(9), 807–813.

Borck, L., Mills, B.J.M., Peeples, M.A., & Clark, J.J. (2015). Are social networks survival networks? An example from the late pre-hispanic US Southwest. *Journal of Archaeological Method and Theory*, 22, 33–57.

Buikstra, J.E. (Ed.) (2019). *Ortner's identification of pathological conditions in human skeletal remains*. Academic Press.

Cohen, M.N., & Armelagos, G.J. (1984). *Paleopathology at the origins of agriculture*. Academic Press.

Cole, G., & Waldron, T. (2019). Cribra orbitalia: Dissecting an ill-defined phenomenon. *International Journal of Osteoarchaeology*, 29(4), 613–621.

Cordell, L. (1997). *Archaeology of the Southwest*: Academic Press.

Cordell, L. S., & McBrinn, M. (2016). *Archaeology of the Southwest*. Routledge.

Crown, P.L. (Ed.) (2000). *Women and men in the prehispanic Southwest: Labor, power, and prestige*. School for Advanced Research.

Da Fonseca, R.R., Smith, B.D., Wales, N., Cappellini, E., Skoglund, P., Fumagalli, M., Samaniego, J.A., Carøe, C., Ávila-Arcos, M.C., Hufnagel, D.E., & Korneliussen, T.S. (2015). The origin and evolution of maize in the

Southwestern United States. *Nature plants*, 1(1), 1–5. DOI: 10.1038/nplants.2014.3.

Dean, J.S., & Van West, C.R. (2002). Environment-behavior relationships in southwestern colorado. In M.D. Varien, and R.H. Wilshusen (Eds.), *Seeking the center place: Archaeology and ancient communities in the mesa verde region* (pp. 81–99). The University of Utah Press.

Driver, J.C. (2002). Faunal variation and change in the Northern San Juan Region. In M.D. Varien, and R.H. Wilshusen (Eds.), *Seeking the center place: Archaeology and ancient communities in the mesa verde region* (pp. 143–160). The University of Utah Press.

Garcia, A.R., Blackwell, A.D., Trumble, B.C., Stieglitz, J., Kaplan, H., & Gurven, M.D. (2020). Evidence for height and immune function tradeoffs among preadolescents in a high pathogen population. *Evolution, Medicine, & Public Health*, 86–99. DOI: 10.1093/emph/eoaa017.

Gómez i Prat, J., & Mendonça de Souza, S.M.F. (2003). Prehistoric tuberculosis in America: Adding comments to a literature review. *Memórias do Instituto Oswaldo Cruz*, 98(Suppl. 1), 151–159. DOI: 10.1590/S0074-02 762003000900023.

Goodman, A.H., Thomas, R.B., Swedlund, A.C., & Armelagos, G.J. (1988). Biocultural perspectives on stress in prehistoric, historical, and contemporary population research. *Yearbook of Physical Anthropology*, 31, 169–202.

Gowland, R. (2015). Entangled lives: Implications of the developmental origins of health and disease hypothesis for bioarchaeology and the life course. *American Journal of Physical Anthropology*, 158, 530–540.

Gravlee, C. (2009). How race becomes biology: Embodiment of social inequality. *American Jourbal of Physical Anthropology*, 139(1), 47–57.

Haas, J., & Creamer, W. (1996). The role of warfare in the Pueblo III period. In M.A. Adler (Ed.), *The prehistoric Pueblo world, AD, 1150* (1350) (pp. 205–213). University of Arizona Press.

Harrod, R.P. (2012). Centers of control: Revealing elites among the Ancestral Pueblo during the "Chaco Phenomenon". *International Journal of Paleopathology*, 2(2–3), 123–135.

Harrod, R.P. (2013). Chronologies of pain and power: Violence, inequality, and social control among Ancestral Pueblo populations (AD 850–1300) (1834). (Doctoral Dissertation, University of Nevada, Las Vegas). UNLV Theses, Dissertations, Professional Papers, and Capstones.

Hill, W.W., & Lange, C.H. (1982). *An ethnography of santa clara pueblo New Mexico*. University of New Mexico Press.

Huff, S., Rudman, D.L., Magalhães, L., Lawson, E., & Kanyamala, M. (2020). Enacting a critical decolonizing ethnographic approach in occupation based research. *Journal of Occupational Science*, 29(1), 115-129. DOI: 10.1080/1442 7591.2020.1824803.

Kantner, J. (2004). *Ancient Puebloan Southwest* (Vol. 5): Cambridge University Press.

Knudson, K.J., & Stojanowski, C.M. (2008). New directions in bioarchaeology: Recent contributions to the study of human social identities. *Journal of Archaeological Research*, 16, 397–432.

Kohler, T.A. (1992). Prehistoric human impact on the environment in the upland North American Southwest. *Population & Environment*, 13(4), 255–268.

Kuckelman, K.A. (2012). Bioarchaeological signatures of Strife in the Northern San Juan. In D.L. Martin, R.P. Harrod, and V.R. Perez (Eds.), *The bioarchaeology of violence* (pp. 121–138). University Press of Florida.

Larsen, C.S. (2015). *Bioarchaeology: Interpreting behavior from the human skeleton*. Cambridge University Press.

LeBlanc, S.A. (1999). *Prehistoric warfare in the American Southwest*. University of Utah Press.

Mann, R.W., & Hunt, D.R. (2013). *Photographic regional atlas of bone disease: A guide to pathologic and normal variation in the human skeleton*. Charles C. Thomas Publisher.

Martin, D.L. (2008). Reanalysis of trauma in the La Plata Valley (900–1300): Strategic social violence and the bioarchaeology of captivity. In A.L.W. Stodder (Ed.), *Reanalysis and reinterpretation in Southwestern bioarchaeology* (pp. 167–184). Arizona State University Anthropological Research Papers No. 59.

Martin, D.L., Akins, N.J., Goodman, A.H., & Swedlund, A.C. (2001). *Harmony and discord: Bioarchaeology of the La Plata Valley*. Museum of New Mexico Press.

Martin, D.L., Goodman, A.H., Armelagos, G.L., & Magennis, A.L. (1991). *Black mesa anasazi health: Reconstructing life from patterns of death and disease* (Vol. 14). Center for Archaeological Investigations, Southern Illinois University.

Martin, D.L., & Osterholtz, A.J. (2016). Broken bodies and broken bones: Biocultural approaches to ancient slavery and torture. In M.K. Zuckerman & D. L. Martin (Eds.), *New directions in biocultural anthropology*, 471–490. Wiley, Blackwell.

Mills, B.J. (2000). Gender, craft production, and inequality. In P. Crown (Ed.), *Women and men in the prehispanic Southwest: Labor, power, and prestige* (pp. 301–343). SAR Press.

New Mexico Department of Health (2018). *2018: The State of health in new Mexico*. New Mexico Department of Health. https://www.nmhealth.org/publication/view/report/4442/

O'Donnell, L. (2019). Indicators of stress and their association with frailty in the precontact Southwestern United States. *American Journal of Physical Anthropology*, 170(3), 404–417.

Ortner, D.J. (2003) *Identification of pathological conditions in human skeletal remains*. Smithsonian Institution Press.

Ortner, D.J., & Putschar, W.G.J. (1981). *Identification of pathological conditions in human skeletal remains*. Smithsonian Institution Press.

Osterholtz, A.J. (2014). Extreme processing at mancos and sacred ridge: The value of comparative studies. In A.J. Osterholtz, K.M. Baustian, and D.L. Martin (Eds.), *Commingled and disarticulated human remains* (pp. 105–127). Springer.

Osterholtz, A.J. (2018). Interpreting and reinterpreting sacred ridge: Placing extreme processing in a larger context. *KIVA*, 84(4), 461–479.

Oxenham, M.F., & Cavill, I. (2010). Porotic hyperostosis and cribra orbitalia: The erythropoietic response to iron-deficiency anaemia. *Anthropological Science*, 118(3), 199–200.

Perry, E.M. (2004). Bioarchaeology of labor and gender in the prehispanic American Southwest. (Doctoral Dissertation, University of Arizona).

Perry, E.M., & Joyce, R.A. (2001). Interdisciplinary applications: Providing a past for "bodies that Matter": Judith Butler's impact on the archaeology of gender. *International Journal of Sexuality and Gender Studies*, 6(1–2), 63–76.

Peterson, K.L. (1988). *Climate and the dolores river anasazi: A paleoenvironmental reconstruction from a 10,000-Year Pollen Record, La Plata Mountains, Southwestern Colorado.* University of Utah Anthropological Papers, no. 113, University of Utah Press.

Potter, J.M., & Chuipka, J. (2007). Early pueblo communities and cultural diversity in the durango area: Preliminary results from the Animas–La Plata project. *Kiva*, 72(4), 407–430.

Rautman, A.E. (1993). Resource variability, risk, and the structure of social networks: An example from the prehistoric Southwest. *American antiquity*, 58(3), 403-424..

Reynolds, A.Z., Wander, K., Sum, C.Y., Su, M., Thompson, M.E., Hooper, P.L., Li, H., Shenk, M.K., Starkweather, K.E., Blumenfield, T., & Mattison, S.M. (2020). Matriliny reverses gender disparities in inflammation and hypertension among the Mosuo of China. *Proceedings of the National Academy of Sciences*, 117(48), 30324-30327. DOI: 10.1073/pnas.2014403117.

Rivera, F., & Mirazón Lahr, M. (2017). New evidence suggesting a dissociated etiology for cribra orbitalia and porotic hyperostosis. *American Journal of Physical Anthropology*, 164(1), 76–96.

Roberts, C.A., & Brickley, M. (2018). Infectious and metabolic diseases: A synergistic relationship. In M.A. Katzenberg, and A.L. Grauer (Eds.), *Biological anthropology of the human skeleton* (pp. 415–446). John Wiley & Sons.

Roberts, C.A., & Buikstra, J.E. (2019). Bacterial infections. In J.E. Buikstra (Ed.), *Ortner's identification of pathological conditions in human skeletal remains* (pp. 321–439). Academic Press.

Roth, B.J. (Ed.) (2010a). *Engendering households in the prehistoric Southwest.* University of Arizona Press.

Roth, B.J. (2010b). Engendering mimbres mogollon pithouse occupations. In B.J. Roth (Ed.), *Engendering households in the prehistoric Southwest* (pp: 136–152). University of Arizona Press.

Rothschild, B., & Jellema, L. (2020). Periosteal reaction recognition and specificity assessed by surface microscopy. *International Journal of Osteoarchaeology*, 30, 355–361. DOI: 10.1002/oa.2864.

Shonkoff, J.P., Garner, A.S., Siegel, B.S., Dobbins, M.I., Earls, M.F., McGuinn, L., Pascoe, J., & Wood, D.L. (2012) Committee on psychosocial aspects of child and family health & committee on early childhood, adoption, and dependent care: The lifelong effects of early childhood adversity and toxic stress. *Pediatrics*, 129(1), e232–e246.

Silko, L.M. (1987). Landscape, history, and the Pueblo imagination. In D. Halpern (Ed.), O*n Nature: Nature, landscape, and natural history* (pp. 83–94). North Point Press.

Sofaer, J.R. (2006). *The body as material culture: A theoretical osteoarchaeology*. Cambridge University Press.

Toll, H.W. (1993). Results of resurvey and evaluation of archaeological sites in the dawson arroyo segment of the La Plata highway project. In *Archaeology notes 67*. Office of Archaeological Studies.

Tuhiwai, S.L. (1999). *Decolonizing methodologies: Research and indigenous peoples*. Zed Books Ltd.

Urlacher, S.S., Ellison, P.T., Sugiyama, L.S., Pontzer, H., Eick, G., Liebert, M.A., Cepon-Robins, T.J., Gildner, T.E., & Snodgrass, J.J. (2018). Tradeoffs between immune function and childhood growth among Amazonian forager-horticulturalists. *Proceedings of the National Academy of Sciences*, 115(17), E3914–E3921.

Varien, M.D. (2010). Depopulation of the Northern San Juan Region: Historical review and archaeological context. In T.A. Kohler, M.D. Varien, and A.M. Wright (Eds.), *Leaving mesa verde: Peril and change in the 13th century southwest* (pp. 1–33). University of Arizona Press.

Varien, M.D., Lipe, W.D., Adler, M.A., Thompson, I.M., & Bradley, B.A. (1996). Southwestern Colorado and southeastern Utah settlement patterns: AD 1100 to 1300 (pp. 86-113). In M.A. Adler (Ed.), *The Prehistoric pueblo world, A.D. 1150-1350* (pp. 86–113). The University of Arizona Press.

Varien, M.D., Ortman, S.G., Kohler, T.A., Glowacki, D.M., & Johnson, C.D. (2007). Historical ecology in the mesa verde region: Results from the village ecodynamics project. *American Antiquity*, 72, 273–299.

Walker, P.L., Bathurst, R.R., Richman, R., Gjerdrum, T., & Andrushko, V. A. (2009). The causes of porotic hyperostosis and cribra orbitalia: A reappraisal of the iron-deficiency-anemia hypothesis. *American Journal of Physical Anthropology*, 139(2), 109–125.

Yaussy, S.L. (2019). The intersections of industrialization: Variation in skeletal indicators of frailty by age, sex, and socioeconomic status in 18th-and 19th-century England. *American Journal of Physical Anthropology*, 170, 116–130.

Zuckerman, M., Harper, K., Barrett, R., & Armelagos, G. (2014). The evolution of disease: Anthropological perspectives on epidemiologic transitions. *Global Health Action*, 7(1), 23303.

Zuckerman, M.K., & Martin, D.L. (Eds.) (2016). *New directions in biocultural anthropology*. John Wiley & Sons.

Zuckerman, M. K., & Crandall, J. (2019). Reconsidering sex and gender in relation to health and disease in bioarchaeology. *Journal of Anthropological Archaeology*, 54, 161–171.

3 Everyday Life Matters: Social Violence at La Plata

Revisiting Violence the Past—Cautionary Notes

Indigenous peoples in the United States have been, and continue to be, subjected to institutionalized forms of violence against their bodies, their psyche, their culture, and their ways of life (Blackhawk, 2009). Their land, resources, children, and livelihoods have been repeatedly stolen from them (Thornton, 1990), and scientists have probed them, studied them, and reduced them to specimens (Deloria, 1997). Accordingly, Indigenous scholars, and others, question the study of violence among non-White groups by White scholars and argue that analyzing and interpreting the violence among Indigenous societies in the past using biased notions and colonial narratives is an extension of settler colonial violence (Blackhawk, 2009; Inwood & Bonds, 2016; Lee, 2014).

It is the intent of this exploration of gender violence in the past to complexify violence, to show how violence is normalized in societies, and how it is meaningful and becomes part of everyday life. Ways of using violence are culturally specific, expressed differently, and perpetrated for different reasons by past and present groups. Most, if not all, cultures practice some form of violence (Ember & Ember, 1997) and in each context, violence is intricately intertwined with cosmologies, ideologies, histories, and masculinities (Martin, 2021).

This volume is a scientific exploration of gendered violence in the past and is somewhat at odds with other narratives about life in the past. For example, Dunbar-Ortiz (2014: 17) presents an overview of health in ancestral Indigenous groups and concludes, based largely on the work of historian Henry Dobyns, that pre-colonial groups "had created a relatively disease-free paradise" and that people "lived long and well." She goes on to explore the role of women in general terms and references journalist Charles C. Mann, who suggested that the

DOI: 10.4324/9781003123521-3

past was a "feminist dream" where women had access to power and control over their own lives (Dunbar-Ortiz, 2014: 17).

Books by Dobyns (1976, 1983) and Mann (2005) present this picture of a feminist paradise in the pre-contact past and the impact of colonialism on native groups; however, these were not data-driven syntheses of what we know about the full lives of people in the past. Historians and journalists rarely access the rich, but often technical archaeological and bioarchaeological literature. Given the lack of engagement with the scientific data on diet, health, and gender roles prior to contact, these volumes tend to present broad generalizing overviews of pre-contact and post-contact Indigenous societies that gloss over culturally specific contexts. To their credit, it serves their purpose to juxtapose the horrors of colonialism against a backdrop of indigenous life as more peaceful, stable, and harmonious. There is no doubt that when compared to precolonial times, settler colonialism practiced by the Spanish, English, and French was genocidal in nature and visited torturous and horrendous atrocities upon Indigenous peoples that persist today, albeit in more covert manifestations. Therefore, while it is not incorrect to say that prior to colonial times, things were better in relation to what was to come with colonial rule and dominance, but it is incorrect to paint the past as peaceful and free of violence, disease, and resource insecurity.

There are many ways to interpret and think about the past, and our reconstruction and analysis here is just one of many ways to piece together likely scenarios that explain the patterns we observe in our studies. While here we base our reconstructions using forensic and bioarchaeological analyses of the physical remains of past peoples and their behaviors, Indigenous scholars like Roxanne Dunbar-Ortiz (2014) provide other ways of understanding the past that are equally as valid and provide important alternative and complementary narratives and ways of thinking about the past. For example, while archaeologists point to data that suggest that the earliest Indigenous peoples entered North America via various routes more than 15,000 years ago (Pringle, 2012; Potter et al., 2018), Indigenous groups have oral traditions and beliefs that affirm that they have been here in the Americas much longer, and in some cases, forever (Steeves, 2021). Therefore, Indigenous groups today have origin stories and cosmological beliefs that are sometimes different, but not necessarily in conflict with the archaeological record.

Both kinds of narratives are important to consider when interpreting the archaeological record, and they are not inherently in conflict with one another because they represent different ways of knowing the past. Kim Tallbear of the University of Alberta and member of the Sisseton Wahpeton Oyatem observes that scientists and journalists tend to focus more on simple and functionalist narratives when they talk about past peoples and the motivations behind their behaviors and choices. She points out that these narratives are reductive, and do not account for the reality that past peoples, who certainly could have been motivated to move around their landscapes because of resource or social stress, were also "fully self-actualized human beings who also had curiosity, who laughed, who had interesting kinship dynamics, who had joy in their lives" (Gannon, 2019, paragraph 38). She suggests that researchers should also consider that past peoples may have migrated for "intellectual reasons or reasons of curiosity" in addition to the search for resources and security (Gannon, 2019, paragraph 38). This is a very important perspective to keep in mind because the archaeological record is fragmentary and sparse, and scientific data is only a partial and narrow view of events and aspects of human life. Indigenous origin narratives and oral traditions provide other ways to conceptualize the range of possibilities for how and why people did what they did thousands of years ago.

With these caveats in mind, in this chapter we present the data on gender violence at La Plata. We propose that gender violence is a very old human behavior and that it was, based on our findings, present in many past populations long before colonial exploitation (Martin & Harrod, 2020). While violence used against Indigenous women is well documented for the colonial period, it is not as well understood in the deeper past prior to contact. The evidence for gender violence is so compelling at La Plata that it has opened up a broader way to conceive of the long history of exploitation and abuse of women, as well as the ways exploited women practiced agency and resistance. In the La Plata case, evidence for trauma is written on the bodies and bones of women who suffered and died young. We explore the biological and archaeological data and offer interpretations about how and why violence was part of everyday life for them.

Why La Plata?

The La Plata communities of the La Plata River Valley are a good case study to discuss how gender violence was entwined with daily life. These communities provide a lens through which gender violence can be perceived from several perspectives: women as wives, women as mothers, women as sisters, and in this case, women as captives and slaves. The roles that these women operated within are complex and challenging to reveal without first-hand accounts or written records. In their ground-breaking study, titled *Mother, Laborer, Captive, Leader,* Harrod and Stone (2018) present a theoretical model for examining the various roles women held among the Ancestral Puebloans in the American Southwest. They provide compelling data derived from a biocultural study of individuals from several archaeological sites and demonstrate how the diversity of identities and roles that women hold and move between are complex but can be reconstructed using fine-grained analyses.

As discussed in Chapter 2, these Ancestral Puebloan groups were living during a turbulent time (ca. AD 900–1350) and offer unique insights into the mechanisms underlying gender violence in a fluctuating and marginal physical environment. Although the La Plata River Valley was comparatively stable and good for agriculture, it was situated in the middle of the Southwest desert region characterized by unreliable rainfall, early and late frosts, and shifting water tables. This scenario is not exceptional or unique to the American Southwest, because as in many parts of the globe farmers continue to be at the mercy of climate fluctuations. With shifts in climate, weather patterns, and soil fertility, there are often periods of food shortages, environmental degradation, and increasing tensions and conflicts. Communities existed for hundreds of years in the La Plata River Valley, and they adjusted to fluctuations in the environment by strategically relocating their communities approximately every 20 years to maximize their access to fertile land. However, even though agricultural output was good for this region, there was still the constant threat of short growing seasons, too little rain, infertile soil, and raiding from neighboring groups (Kohler & Turner, 2006).

This chapter is an overview of the body politic, a theoretical approach that invites us to see violence in a broader, more meaningful context, and a presentation of the empirical data on violence against women at La Plata. Using standard bioarchaeological and forensic techniques, we argue that the skeletal and mortuary data suggests gender violence at La Plata was part of a broader strategy of raiding and abduction of women and children from neighboring groups, who then became indentured servants within their captor's households. We discuss the clinical consequences of the observed healed trauma among individuals at La Plata, focusing particularly on individuals exhibiting healed cranial wounds and the neuropsychological consequences of those injuries, which we argue may have predisposed them to repeated experiences of violence.

The Body Politic: Wounds to the Body and Power

In the analysis of gender violence at La Plata, we want to remind the reader to think of violence against women at La Plata in terms of the three-body framework discussed in Chapter 1. This theoretical framework provides a way to complexify the layered and nuanced effects of violence against women to understand its impact. Through a variety of forensic and bioarchaeological methods, we show how the individual body provides basic information on age-at-death, osteological sex, health, activity patterns, and experiences of traumatic injury. The social body is reflected in skeletal signatures of diet, metabolic and infectious disease, and traumatic injuries and alterations to the skeleton due to behavioral and cultural activities. At La Plata, we show that the communities living there experienced several health problems typical of desert agriculturalists in the region and associated with individual age, sex, gender, and life history. We discuss how observed patterns in skeletal data at the individual and population-level are a product of social processes informing the division of daily tasks and performance of culturally and socially defined roles.

The third body in the three-body framework is the body politic, in which we contextualize the observed patterns of health, disease, workloads, and trauma on the skeletal remains to identify the social and political processes structuring differential treatment and experiences of social violence between individuals at La Plata. Drawing on a wide range of bioarchaeological and historical literature and forensic cases, Martin et al. (2010) identified ways that human groups politicize and use violence, and the skeletal correlates or signatures of these different types of violence, summarized in Figure 3.1. The skeletal signatures of violence can look different depending on the type of violence being perpetrated (e.g. food restriction vs. massacre). However injuries to the head, face, and neck are the most obvious and common evidence of lived experiences of violence used to keep subgroups of individuals in subordinate and submissive social positions (Brink, 2009). We discuss the patterns of cranial trauma observed among a subgroup of adult women at La Plata in reference to the skeletal signatures of different types of cultural and social violence summarized in Figure 3.1 to show how these women were embedded within a system of social violence meant to keep them in subordinate and submissive social positions.

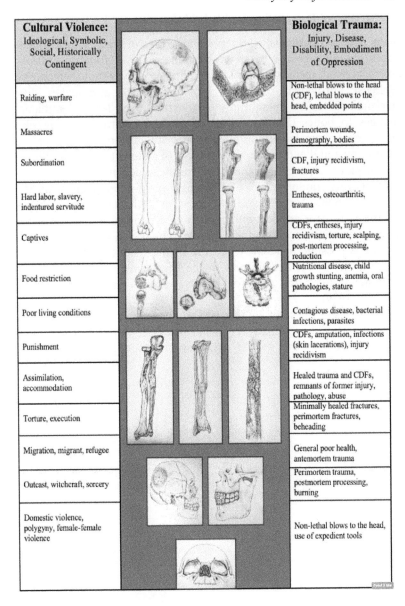

Cultural Violence: Ideological, Symbolic, Social, Historically Contingent	Biological Trauma: Injury, Disease, Disability, Embodiment of Oppression
Raiding, warfare	Non-lethal blows to the head (CDF), lethal blows to the head, embedded points
Massacres	Perimortem wounds, demography, bodies
Subordination	CDF, injury recidivism, fractures
Hard labor, slavery, indentured servitude	Entheses, osteoarthritis, trauma
Captives	CDFs, entheses, injury recidivism, torture, scalping, post-mortem processing, reduction
Food restriction	Nutritional disease, child growth stunting, anemia, oral pathologies, stature
Poor living conditions	Contagious disease, bacterial infections, parasites
Punishment	CDFs, amputation, infections (skin lacerations), injury recidivism
Assimilation, accommodation	Healed trauma and CDFs, remnants of former injury, pathology, abuse
Torture, execution	Minimally healed fractures, perimortem fractures, beheading
Migration, migrant, refugee	General poor health, antemortem trauma
Outcast, witchcraft, sorcery	Perimortem trauma, postmortem processing, burning
Domestic violence, polygyny, female-female violence	Non-lethal blows to the head, use of expedient tools

Figure 3.1 Types of cultural violence and their skeletal signatures discussed in Martin et al. (2010). Illustrations by Claira Ralston.

Identifying and Interpreting the Skeletal Correlates of Violence

Being able to distinguish the types and causes of trauma to people's bones has long been a focus of bioarchaeologists, forensic anthropologists, and medical clinicians. Philip Walker, a noted bioarchaeologist, provided methods and theoretical approaches for investigating violent intent and the ways that it can leave identifiable changes to bones (Walker, 2001). Using a biocultural framework, many researchers have continued to develop methods for correctly identifying and diagnosing different types of trauma to bone, and how to interpret their social meaning (Martin & Anderson, 2014).

Identifying trauma in the osteological record is relatively straightforward. Applied force leaves permanent and unique changes on bone when that force is applied with enough power to cause tissue damage that penetrates through skin and muscle to bone. Evidence of survived trauma is possible to identify because of the unique ways that bone responds to injury, and injuries to the head leave particularly characteristic lesions that last for many years (Figures 3.2 and 3.3) (Walker, 1989).

The bones of the skull are thin and composed of an inner and outer layer of cortical bone, in-between which is a layer of porous trabecular bone. Figure 3.2 shows several ways that the bones of the cranial vault

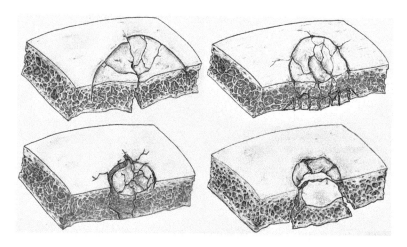

Figure 3.2 Illustrations of unhealed cranial depression fractures depicting some of the ways that the bones of the cranial vault bend and break in response to blunt trauma. Adapted from Moritz, 1954: 344. Illustrations by Claira Ralston.

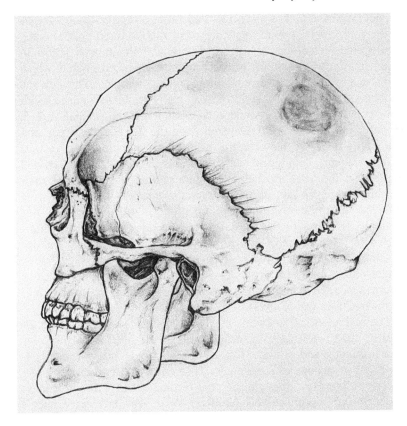

Figure 3.3 Illustration of an antemortem cranial depression fracture to the left parietal bone. Illustration by Claira Ralston.

can bend and break when hit with a blunt object. If the membranes that cover the brain are not breached, it is possible for the victim to survive the trauma and the cranial fracture to heal. If the cranial fracture is allowed to heal, the impact site typically remains permanently depressed. These depressions, called cranial depression fractures (CDFs), are visible and often palpable throughout the rest of an individual's life (Figure 3.3).

Cranial depression fractures are produced when a blunt force is applied to one side of the bone. The outer layer of bone is depressed inward, displacing and depressing the underlying trabecular layer. As the outer layer continues to depress the trabecular layer, the outer layer of bone slowly deforms and ultimately fails, producing characteristic concentric and radiating fracture paths from the point of impact (Wedel & Galloway, 2013). This process ruptures blood vessels in the trabecular layer and periosteum of the fractured cranial bone, producing a hematoma six to eight hours after the injury is inflicted. The hematoma is gradually replaced by new connective tissue, which forms a fibrous callous around the fractured margins. Through the process of remodeling, this fibrous callous is gradually replaced with new bone, leaving a permanent depression on the cranial surface (Figure 3.3) (Nolan, 2005). Depending on the size of the weapon and the strength of the blow to the head, depression fractures can be variable in size, depth, and shape. Patterns in the location of cranial depression fractures are helpful in interpreting the nature of their production, which can inform the circumstances wherein they were received and the motivations of the perpetrators of the violence. For example, fractures to the frontal or facial bones are generally inter-preted to be reflective of face-to-face interpersonal violence (e.g. do-mestic abuse, interpersonal conflict) (Lambert, 1997; Walker, 2001), whereas fractures to the posterior cranium are generally interpreted as injuries received while running away (e.g. raiding, captive taking) (Walker, 2001; Webb, 1995).

The body politic framework helps us to connect skeletal evidence of trauma due to violence with social processes and institutions of power that normalize and promote the use of violence against particular in-dividuals or groups of individuals. Through this framework, we ask questions like: How does violence and trauma to the bodies of women produce and reproduce social power? Who benefits from women's subordination and subservience? In what ways do trauma to the head and body contribute to enforcing a particular social hierarchy? Individuals that are subjected to and controlled with physical trauma are often beaten about the head, which confuses, disorients, and in-capacitates the victim, rendering them more passive and pliable.

In the remainder of this chapter, we present a bioarchaeological analysis of the individuals recovered from La Plata and situate their biological and mortuary data within its culturally and politically spe-cific context to illustrate the variable role violence played in women's daily lives and deaths within these communities.

Captives as Disposable Commodities: The Evidence for Violence, Illness, Heavy Labor, and Early Death

As discussed in Chapter 2, the La Plata River Valley was home to many small communities situated along the La Plata River in what is now northern New Mexico. It was a permanently watered and quite productive agricultural area in which more than 900 sites have been reported. To recap, the valley was continuously occupied from AD 200 until AD 1300. This area was lush by local and regional standards, and the density of available agricultural and wild resources was high. These communities were also beneficially situated between the socio-political and economic hubs centered on the Mesa Verde region to the north and Chaco Canyon to the south, embedding them within rich and dynamic socio-political, economic, and ideological interaction spheres. Trade items and nonutilitarian goods were found in La Plata sites, suggesting that communities within and beyond the valley were connected through trade, exchange, and raiding/warfare. Although skeletal indicators of health suggest a comparatively robust and healthy population for the American Southwest, there is also evidence of sustained violence against a subgroup of predominantly female individuals within the La Plata communities. These individuals are the focus of this interpretive study.

The methods for the analysis of trauma on cranial and post-cranial remains follow the recommendations of Wedel and Galloway (2013) in this discussion of the individuals living at La Plata. Evidence for trauma in the La Plata burial series focuses on the injuries that adult females living within these communities survived. Antemortem trauma (trauma occurring a period of time prior to death) refers to healed or healing fractures and other injuries to the skeleton that are macroscopically identifiable on skeletal remains and represent episodes of survived trauma and, in most circumstances, forms of violence. While antemortem injuries were nonlethal, they still reflect a burden of suffering that particular individuals in these communities sustained.

Skeletal Trauma at La Plata

A total of 51 individuals could be evaluated for healed cranial and post-cranial traumatic injuries at La Plata, and of these there were antemortem fractures to both the cranial and postcranial body in adults of all ages (Table 3.1). Of the 14 women that could be evaluated for cranial trauma, five exhibited antemortem cranial depression fractures and received seemingly careless burial treatment (sprawled or semi-flexed arrangements), and one woman with cranial trauma that could not be assigned to a mortuary condition. Six women exhibited no antemortem cranial trauma and were intentionally buried in flexed or semi-flexed positions with associated grave goods, one woman with no cranial trauma was arranged in a semi-flexed position but was not

Table 3.1 Summary of individuals with cranial and postcranial trauma at La Plata

Burial	Age/Sex	Cranial	Postcranial
37592 B6	15	Left parietal, 7 × 12 mm depression fracture	Right fibula, healed fracture
37593 B5	? F		Right rib 6, left rib 9 healed fractures, thoracic vertebrae 8 and 9 wedge fractures, and osteophyte development
37593 B3	48 M		Right 1st metacarpal healed fracture
37599 B4	45 M		Right radius and ulna distal ends with remodeled, misshapen lesions; healed Colle's fracture
37599 B5	25 M	Right parietal, 30 × 30 mm depression fracture (partly ununited)	Right scapula, roughened depression near scapular spine; right ribs 6 and 7 and left rib 8 healed fractures, remodeled with palpable depression; C3–5 trauma-induced osteophytes; L1 healed fracture
37599 B9	25 M	Left frontal, orbit 6 × 9 mm depression fracture	
37600 B4	50 M		
37601 B4	25 F	Left parietal and center on frontal bone above orbits, 6+ well-rounded depression fractures ranging in size	
37601 B5	35 M	Left parietal near occipital 20 × 15 mm depression fracture	
37601 B10	38 F	Right frontal above orbit 9 × 5 mm depression fracture with dense bone and depressed ring	
37603 B2.1	30 F		Right radius, healed Colle's fracture
65030 B6	38 F	Occipital 24 × 24 mm depression fracture	Left hip, acetabulum, and neighboring area osteophyte development
65030 B8	20 F	Right and left nasals, healed broken nose	C1 and C2 healed fractures
65030 B9	33 F	At bregma, 57 × 77mm area with large bump, sutures ununited	Left pelvis, fracture to pubic plate
65030 B16	28 F	Right frontal 17 × 17mm depression fracture, occipital 7 × 7 mm depression fracture	

buried with any grave offerings, and finally one men with no cranial trauma whose original mortuary treatment could not be determined.

Comparatively, men with and without observable cranial and post-cranial trauma at La Plata exhibited more variability in mortuary treatment than women. Of the 14 men that could be assessed for cranial trauma, six exhibited no cranial trauma and were buried arranged in a flexed position with grave goods, five exhibited no cranial trauma but were not buried with grave goods and were arranged in a variety of positions ranging from extended to flexed. Finally, of the three males who exhibited cranial trauma, one was buried with grave goods, and two were not, although all three were arranged in a semi-flexed position indicating intential graves.

For the six women with antemortem cranial trauma, the observed depression fractures were generally concentrated around the top, front, and back of the cranium (frontal and occipital bones), whereas men tended to exhibit slightly more variety in trauma location, with fractures occurring to the frontal and occipital bones, but also to the parietals. The cranial injuries observed are consistent with the definition of cranial depression fractures produced by blows to the head sustained in violent encounters (Ali & Badar, 2021). The variation in the overall size and dimensions of the cranial depression fractures observed on the La Plata individuals suggests that any number of different implements could have been used to produce these fractures. In their review of artifacts associated with warfare and hand combat, Wilcox and Haas (1994: 223–224) find little evidence for the manufacture of objects solely to be used as weapons, so it is difficult to verify exactly what type of implement was used in each case of cranial trauma at La Plata, but modern forensic studies suggest that cranial fractures can be produced with a wide range of blunt or sharp implements (Kranioti, 2015).

While it is easy to envision a stone axe, hammerstone, core, chopper, or projectile point producing skeletal trauma, it is equally likely that bone, antler, and wood objects could be used as well. For example, a forensic case involving cranial and post-cranial wounds like those at La Plata was produced when an individual was repeatedly struck with a common wooden yard broom (Bhootra, 1985), which is not unlike the size, shape, and weight of a Pueblo digging stick (Colton, 1960: 96). Digging sticks were likely common and in abundant supply in agricultural communities like the sites at La Plata. Colton (1960: 98) states that wooden digging sticks occasionally had a hoe made of hafted stone, or triangular pieces of basalt or sandstone. Thinking about the types of technologies that people used hundreds of years ago in the La

Plata River Valley, most expedient weapons were likely fashioned from everyday implements used in agriculture or hunting, like digging sticks, stone tools, hammerstones, and axes. While bow and arrow technology was used for hunting, the types of trauma observed on the La Plata individuals are more consistent with injuries inflicted by blunt objects like stone axes, ground stones, and wooden clubs.

There is a marked difference in the frequency of antemortem cranial and postcranial trauma between adult men and women at La Plata. Women are three times more likely to experience cranial trauma than men (14.2% men versus 42.8% women) and women were twice as likely to experience post-cranial trauma than adult men (18.7% men versus 35.7% women). The frequencies of antemortem trauma among adults at La Plata greatly outnumber those for subadults, who have an overall rate of 4.7% for cranial trauma and virtually no cases of post-cranial trauma.

Among men, there are three cases of antemortem cranial trauma: one 25-year-old exhibits a healed compression fracture to the right parietal; another 25-year-old presents with a healed depressed fracture to the corner of the left orbit; and a 35-year-old individual exhibits a healed depression fracture to the left parietal bone. Post-cranial fractures among La Plata men include a healed Colle's fracture to the right radius and ulna (typically produced by falling onto an outstretched arm) in a 50-year-old, a healed fracture to the right thumb (hallux) in a 45-year-old, and one 48-year-old menobserved among adult males at La who presented with several healed rib and vertebrae fractures. The post-cranial fractures observed among adult men at La Plata did not co-occur with any cranial trauma and are consistent with traumatic injuries sustained in occupation-related or accidental circumstances (e.g. hunting, falls, etc.) (Wedel & Galloway, 2013).

Skeletal Trauma at La Plata: Victims of Violence?

Of the 14 women examined in this study, six individuals between the ages of 20 and 38 years recovered from contexts dating to the PII (1000–1125) (n = 1) (LA 65030 B16) and PIII (AD 11250–1300) (n = 5) periods exhibit antemortem cranial trauma. The inventory of healed nonlethal cranial wounds for women at La Plata is more extensive than that of men, with three of the six cases among the women involving multiple head wounds (injury recidivism). A 25-year-old adult woman (LA 37601 B4) exhibits multiple depression fractures to the front and side of the head (Figure 3.4). The youngest woman (LA 65030 B8, age 20) exhibits a healed broken nose and crushing injuries to the first and

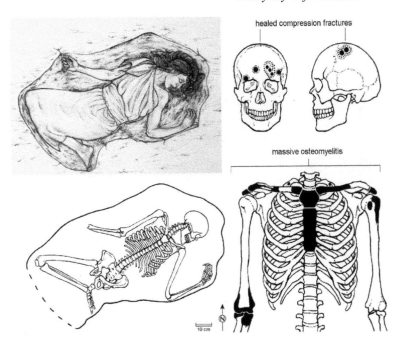

Figure 3.4 Woman, age 25 (LA 37601 B4). Burial context reconstruction and line drawings detailing body position and cranial trauma and postcranial pathology. (Burial reconstruction by Claira Ralston. Line drawings courtesy of Robert Turner, Office of Archaeological Studies, Department of Cultural Affairs, Santa Fe, NM).

second cervical vertebrae of the neck (Figure 3.5), a 33-year-old woman (LA 65030 B9) exhibits a large, un-reunited but healed series of severe fractures to the top of the head (Figure 3.6), and one 28-year-old (LA 65030 B16) presents with a fracture above the right orbit and to the back of the head (Figure 3.7). Finally, a 38-year-old woman (LA 37601 B10) has a healed fracture above the right orbit, and a second 38-year-old (LA 65030 B6) exhibits a depression fracture to the back of the head (Figure 3.8).

Four of the six woman with antemortem cranial trauma also experienced postcranial trauma, and four of the six also exhibited lesions consistent with metabolic stress (e.g. porotic hyperostosis) and/or infection (e.g. periosteal reaction, osteomyelitis). In addition to the multiple depression fractures to their cranium, the 25-year-old individual (LA 37601 B4) exhibits well-healed antemortem fractures to the right shoulder, several right and left ribs, the first lumbar vertebra, and

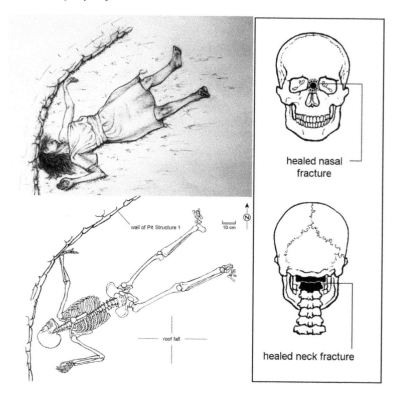

Figure 3.5 Woman, age 20 (LA 65030 B8). Burial context reconstruction and line drawings detailing body position and cranial trauma. (Burial reconstruction by Claira Ralston. Line drawings courtesy of Robert Turner, Office of Archaeological Studies, Department of Cultural Affairs, Santa Fe, NM).

possible trauma-induced osteophytic development on the third, fourth, and fifth cervical vertebrae of the neck. This individual also presented with a severe case of osteomyelitis that affected numerous postcranial elements. Osteomyelitis is a painful bone infection caused by bacteria or fungi introduced into bone tissues, causing inflammation in the bone marrow and on the bone surface (periosteum), and can destroy and occasionally cause bone death (necrosis) if left untreated (Ortner, 2003: 179–206). Parts of this individual's sternum, right and left scapula, right and left clavicles, proximal left humerus, distal right humerus, and proximal right radius and ulna exhibit circumscribed lesions of thickened, swollen-looking reactive bone deposits. These lesions are characterized by raised areas of periosteal reaction and cloacal openings

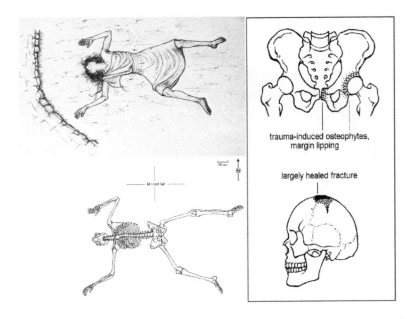

Figure 3.6 Woman, age 33 (LA 65030 B9). Burial context reconstruction and line drawings detailing body position and cranial and postcranial trauma. (Burial reconstruction by Claira Ralston. Line drawings courtesy of Robert Turner, Office of Archaeological Studies, Department of Cultural Affairs, Santa Fe, NM).

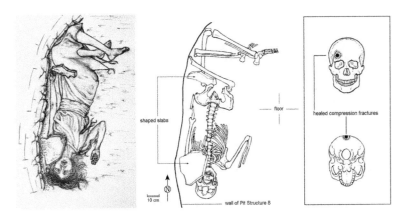

Figure 3.7 Female, age 38 (LA 65030 B16). Burial context reconstruction and line drawings detailing body position and cranial trauma. (Burial reconstruction by Claira Ralston. Line drawings courtesy of Robert Turner, Office of Archaeological Studies, Department of Cultural Affairs, Santa Fe, NM).

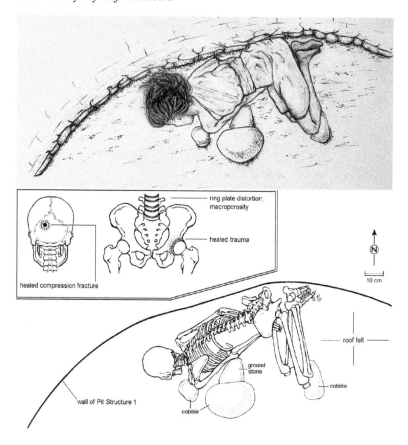

Figure 3.8 Woman, age 38 (LA 65030 B6). Burial context reconstruction and line drawings detailing body position and cranial and postcranial trauma. (Burial reconstruction by Claira Ralston. Line drawings courtesy of Robert Turner, Office of Archaeological Studies, Department of Cultural Affairs, Santa Fe, NM).

(drainage channels for pus), which are interspersed with sequestered areas of necrotic bone and bone surfaces that appear smooth and rounded, all of which are produced by osteolytic and sclerotic bone deposition processes consistent with osteomyelitis (Mann & Hunt, 2005: 153–155; Ortner & Putschar, 1985: 105–111).

The pus-producing bacteria (e.g. *staphylococcus aureus*) that cause osteomyelitis can reach the skeleton via direct infection from a traumatic wound, from infections that start in the skin and gradually expand to the bone surface, or by vascular routes originating from a point of initial infection (Cleveland Clinic, 2021). Although we cannot definitively determine the source of the massive infection affecting this individual's shoulders and chest area, the localized nature of the infection begs the question: What likely caused this? Given that this individual also experienced antemortem fractures to their scapulae, several ribs, and cervical vertebrae, it is possible that this localized infection may have been caused by the traumatic event that produced the postcranial injuries, either by a penetrating injury that impacted a bone or through an infected skin wound in the general area.

In addition to a healed broken nose and possible traumatic injuries to the first and second cervical vertebrae, the 20-year-old woman (LA 65030 B8) also presented with healed lesions on cranial and postcranial elements suggestive of metabolic stress and infection (i.e. porotic hyperostosis and periosteal reaction). The 33-year-old woman with severe trauma to the top of the head (LA 65030 B9) also exhibited a healed fracture to the left pelvis, but no other pathological lesions. And finally, the 38-year-old woman (LA 65030 B6) exhibits a probable fracture and trauma-induced osteoarthritic changes to the left hip joint, healed porotic hyperostosis lesions, and areas of active periosteal reaction.

Antemortem postcranial trauma is also present on two other woman from the La Plata Sites who do not exhibit antemortem cranial trauma: one individual of undetermined age (LA 37592 B5) has a healed fracture to the right fibula, and a 30-year-old who exhibits a healed Colle's fracture to the distal right radius. While this suggests that both men and women at La Plata were at risk for experiencing postcranial trauma, the co-occurrence of both cranial and postcranial trauma and injury recidivism among the younger women, and the presence of lesions consistent with metabolic disease and infections among four of the six women discussed above sets them apart from the rest of the La Plata burial population.

Evidence of Heavy Labor at La Plata

Several of the women with antemortem cranial trauma also have patterns of nonpathological lesions and skeletal changes associated with occupational stress and habitual use of particular muscle groups. For example, both women in Pit structure 1 from site LA 65030 (B8 and B9) (Figures 3.5 and 3.6) demonstrate asymmetrical robusticity for many of the length and width proportions of their long bones, with the humerus, radius, and ulna being the most affected. Trinkaus et al. (1994) have demonstrated that bilateral humeral asymmetry in extant and extinct groups is correlated with repetitive and activity-specific biomechanical changes to bone (i.e. entheses), therefore the asymmetries in robusticity observed among these individuals suggest that they likely engaged in the performance of strenuous and repetitive activities utilizing the major muscle groups of the upper extremity. Several of these individuals also have pronounced cases of ossified ligaments and localized enthesopathies at major muscle attachment sites on their humeri, radii, and ulnae, as well as osteophytic development along the margins of postcranial joint surfaces. As a group, these women are generally too young to have naturally developed the osteophytic developments and osteoarthritic changes typically associated with aging, therefore the observed osteophytic changes are more likely related to extensive and repetitive use of certain muscle groups that resulted in the build-up of bone and degenerative change at sites undergoing extensive biomechanical stress.

Although the subgroup sample size limits a detailed quantitative analysis of occupational stress markers, it is possible to speculate a division of labor by sex and "status" at La Plata. Spencer and Jennings (1965), Titiev (1972), Dozier (1970) describe sexual divisions of labor among the Pueblo peoples, where Pueblo women were generally responsible for grinding corn, preparing meals, carrying water, gathering wild food resources and maintaining the household gardens, building and mending houses, and making pottery, baskets, and clothing. Pueblo men were primarily responsible for farming, hunting, long-distance trade, weaving, and performing religious and ceremonial activities. The task of grinding a season's crop of corn into meal to be stored for the year belonged exclusively to women, who could spend as many as eight to nine hours a day at the grindstone for several weeks to prepare meals for their households and community-wide ceremonial uses and feasting activities (see Chapter 4). Therefore, based on ethnographic and ethnohistoric correlates and the osteological changes observed in the upper extremities, in particular, it is reasonable to assume that these individuals likely participated in repetitive activities that engaged the muscle groups of the upper extremity (e.g. grinding corn, carrying heavy loads, etc.).

Mortuary Treatment at La Plata

The way in which the six women with antemortem cranial and postcranial injuries were buried also distinguishes them from other women and men at La Plata who did not exhibit cranial trauma. During the PII and PIII periods, the standard mortuary treatment of deceased adult individuals in the La Plata River Valley was intentional inhumation in abandoned structures, storage pits, or prepared shallow

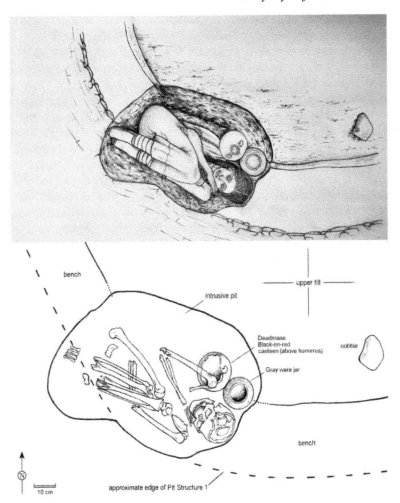

Figure 3.9 Woman, age 25 (LA 37595 B1). Burial context reconstruction and line drawing representing the typical mortuary pattern at La Plata, where the individual is intentionally placed in a defined shallow pit, usually with offerings. (Burial reconstruction by Claira Ralston. Line drawing courtesy of Robert Turner, Office of Archaeological Studies, Department of Cultural Affairs, Santa Fe, NM).

pits within middens with the body intentionally arranged in flexed or semi-flexed position with grave offerings of ceramics, small clay objects, stone tools and ground stones deliberately placed and arranged around the body (Figure 3.9).

None of the six adult women at La Plata who exhibited antemortem cranial trauma were buried in the typical pattern. All were found in positions that can be described as loosely flexed, prostrate, haphazard, or sprawled as if they were thrown or tossed into abandoned pit structures, and none were buried with grave offerings (Figures 3.4–3.8).

Notably, three of the six individuals were found in the lower fill of an abandoned pit structure and appear to have all died at approximately the same time and were disposed of together. These include two adult women aged 20 (LA 65030 B8) and 33 (LA 65030 B9) and an 11-year-old child (LA 65030 B7) (Figure 3.10). All are in a haphazard position as if thrown into the pit structure from a higher elevation. We cannot know for sure if these individuals represent two sisters and one of their children, a mother and her child and an unrelated women, two unrelated women and a child taken captive from the same community, or some other combination of relationships, but the context does suggest that these individuals were related.

Survivors of Violence: The Long-Term Effects of Cranial Trauma

For individuals who have sustained and survived injuries to the head, there are short-and long-term physiological and neurological consequences that are collectively referred to as traumatic brain injuries (TBI). The primary damage occurs on impact and initiates a cascading sequence of physical and neurological changes (Bernert & Turski, 1996; Sarvghad-Moghaddam et al., 2014). The following section is taken largely from our earlier work into the neurological effects of TBI on behavior (see Martin et al., 2008).

The force of a blow to the skull is initially imparted to the underlying brain tissue, which absorbs and rebounds in response to the force of the blow similar to the way a soccer ball behaves when it is kicked: the brain bounces away from the point of impact (the *coup*), and then strikes the inside of the cranial vault 180 degrees from the original site of impact (the *contrecoup*). In most circumstances the *contrecoup* produces a more severe injury to the brain than the trauma inflicted to the brain at the initial site of impact (the *coup*). Additionally, because the brain is completely contained within the cranial vault, if the force of impact is powerful enough, the brain can continue to rebound within the bony vault along multiple axes, essentially ricocheting from one interior boney wall to another. As it bounces internally, the soft tissues of the brain are stretched and compressed by radiating shock waves, a process called *shearing*, which continues to inflict secondary traumatic injuries to the brain.

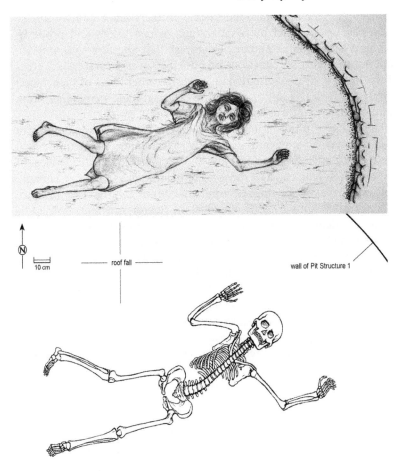

N

10 cm — roof fall — wall of Pit Structure 1

Figure 3.10 Child, age 11 (LA 65030 B7). No trauma or pathology. Buried in the same pit structure with the women in Figures 3.5 and 3.6. (Burial reconstruction by Claira Ralston. Line drawing courtesy of Robert Turner, Office of Archaeological Studies, Department of Cultural Affairs, Santa Fe, NM).

Unlike the primary injuries produced by the initial impact, which occur within a relatively brief period, secondary injuries can produce physiological and neurological effects that last for prolonged, indefinite periods time. For instance, the brain may continue to swell after the initial impact in response to the physical trauma, but because the brain is enclosed within the boney cranial vault, the resulting edema produces increasing intracranial pressure that compresses the soft neuronal brain tissues against the inside of the skull, inflicting further injury. Similarly, blood vessels on the surface and within the brain can be ruptured by blunt trauma, which bleeds and produces localized hemorrhages and/or hematomas that interfere with and disrupt normal neuronal functions because they over-saturate some areas of the brain with pooled blood and deprive other areas of their blood supply (hypoxia), resulting in neuron-cell death and permanent brain damage (Bernert & Turski, 1996; Hohlrieder et al., 2003).

The range of physical and behavioral changes that can result from head trauma is significant. Generally, a traumatic brain injury will present with an initial, transient loss of consciousness or extended loss of consciousness (e.g. coma) if the force of the trauma is extensive enough. Following the initial impact, traumatic brain injuries can produce complex alterations to different types of neurological functions. For instance, a depression fracture to the left temporal/parietal region may impair speech production and weaken the ability of an individual to manipulate their right arm but leave his or her left arm unaffected. Vision and balance can be compromised by a blow to the back of the head, but hearing remains intact. A blow to the orbit region can compromise cranial nerves and produce diplopia (double vision) and facial paresthesia or paralysis depending on the location of the fracture. Head trauma can also predispose individuals to persistent migraines, impaired memory formation, impaired ability to sustain attention, compromised language processing and word formation, damaged visual-spatial comprehension and balance, hearing loss, and facial and tongue paralysis where an individual can no longer emote or verbally communicate effectively (Katzen et al., 2003; Parikh et al., 2007).

Behavioral changes stemming from both initial and secondary traumatic brain injuries are categorized depending on what parts of the brain have been affected, including areas responsible for controlling certain skills, like language processing, communication, memory retention, concentration, motor skills, or those controlling emotion and personality. In general, the most common changes in mental status following a traumatic head injury are amnesia, impairment in concentration and motivation, agitation, and disinhibition/impulsivity (Parikh et al., 2007). After a closed head injury, victims may still be able to maintain focus on something that interests them, but they cannot sustain their focus for operational lengths of time. They may also experience impairments in levels of awareness as well. People who sustain concussions, for instance, find that they may suddenly lose mindfulness in social situations, or their mental clarity and acuity is dulled, akin to the physiological effects of intoxication. Similarly, some may experience onsets of epileptic seizures, which can also introduce profound alterations to mental status

(Diaz-Arrastia et al., 2000), and changes in mood (i.e. acute depression and anxiety) (Holsinger et al., 2002).

Changes in social and emotional behavior are common among individuals who sustain TBIs, who are also more likely to experience and exhibit disinhibitions in aggressive behavior and/or sexual appetites (Milders et al., 2003). In general, people who are aggressive in social contexts and who misinterpret (or ignore) social cues are at greater risk of experiencing additional cranial and postcranial injuries. In the context of La Plata, it is worth noting that several of the individuals with cranial trauma also exhibit injury recidivism, or repeated sequences of healed cranial and postcranial injuries that were inflicted at different times. It is possible that these individuals' repeated experiences of violence and traumatic injury may have been a consequence of behavioral issues, functional deficiencies, and/or complications with social competencies arising due to complications from the cranial trauma they experienced. Therefore, victims of violence that produced significant cranial trauma may have technically survived their injuries, but they likely continued to experience a range of long-lasting physiological and neurological effects on their cognitive and emotional wellbeing that may have predisposed them to continued experiences of violence over their lifetimes.

Summary: Culturally Specific Gender Violence at La Plata

As we demonstrated above, a subgroup of women in the communities of the La Plata River Valley bore an unequal burden of traumatic injuries to their bodies compared to other women and men. Furthermore, the co-occurrence of antemortem cranial and post-cranial trauma, infections, and overall decreased life expectancy (i.e. there were very few old adult women represented in the burial assemblage) suggest comparatively bleak social circumstances for a subgroup of women in these communities. Women exhibiting antemortem cranial and postcranial trauma and other indicators of metabolic and disease stress were more likely to be individuals who received expedient mortuary treatment, with their bodies haphazardly thrown or discarded into convenient pits with no associated grave offerings. As a group, this particular subgroup has six women who were young relative to other women at these sites who exhibited no trauma and received normative, intentionally prepared burial treatment.

If the La Plata River Valley was doing so well with agricultural production and population increases, why was there a subgroup of women who were fairing so poorly? What is the relationship between wealth and power on one hand, and suffering and disability on the other? Standard economic models applied to precolonial groups that search for meaning within a local context tend to miss the complex patterns that exist. Violence against women in an area where there was an abundance of resources makes sense only if a regional model of shifting political and economic strategies is also considered. While their world was becoming increasingly connected, it may not have been necessarily unified. The dynamics of social change at La Plata may have taken place in an arena of increasing relationships defined by domination and accommodation or resistance, and as more people moved into the La Plata Valley, it is possible that members of the local community increasingly controlled and restricted access to productive agricultural resources to select groups of individuals. Therefore, health, disease, and trauma at La Plata, with its abundant agricultural and wild resources, cannot be understood without looking at the local and regional dynamics involving the control of those resources and the productive labor force (e.g. women) required to produce and accumulate those resources. It is likely that as the La Plata River Valley population increased (through a combination of immigration and increased fertility), several things may have occurred. It may have been necessary to increase the production of food to feed the growing numbers of people living within the communities, and therefore a need for more productive laborers.

In agricultural-subsistence societies, agricultural intensification was often accompanied by a concomitant pressure on women to increase their economic productivity while simultaneously decreasing birth spacing (Harris & Ross, 1987: 49). This situation places an enormous labor burden on women, who must partition their time, energy, and activities between different and often competing tasks: economic labor and everyday household tasks, and bearing, breastfeeding, and rearing small children. Harris and Ross cite summary data (1987: 50) on the number of hours that women labor daily in agricultural villages and found that women work between 6.7 and 10.8 hours a day accomplishing their required daily labor tasks.

Therefore, reproductive-aged women would be the most advantageous group to exploit for productive labor because they could aid in domestic tasks and food production, as well as in child-rearing. This would not necessarily rule out the exploitation of men as well, although they tended to be killed in raiding activities rather than taken as captives (see Chapter 4).

Raiding for women and children in this region of the American Southwest has been extensively discussed by archaeologists like Tim Kohler and Christie Turner (2006) and Catherine Cameron (2016),

Indigenous historians and scholars like Ned Blackhawk (2009), Andrés Reséndez (2016), and Gonzales and Lamadrid (2019), and James Brooks (2011). For example, using published data on the age-at-death and sex of adult burials across the American Southwest, Kohler and Turner (2006) found that at some locations there were more female burials than males and they hypothesized that this pattern was best explained by raiding activities and the capture of females. They found that in the AD 1200s the La Plata River Valley and surrounding areas had more females than expected if the sex ratios in any given community approached 50/50. With an overabundance of adult females and fewer than expected males in the community cemeteries, the most likely explanation is that there were captive females in some communities who elevated the ratio of the number of females relative to males. Therefore, the communities at La Plata may have felt it necessary to construct rigid rules about resource allocation and may have chosen a strategy that utilized captives to work the land and increase their household and agricultural economies.

The picture of La Plata that emerges from this discussion is one of an agricultural population that was doing relatively well given the circumstances of crowded living and subsistence farming in a desert environment. Anemia and infectious disease are expected outcomes of groups utilizing agrarian lifeways, however the morbidity burdens common among societies practicing these lifeways in the past are not as pronounced as expected at La Plata. In comparison to nearby communities in the Mesa Verde and Chaco Canyon regions, La Plata individuals appeared to be faring comparatively well. However, this is overshadowed by the high frequencies of trauma found in the women featured in this discussion. The high frequencies of cranial trauma and other co-morbidities observed among the six adult women discussed above reflect that, at least for a small subgroup of individuals living at La Plata, that violence was present and embedded within daily life, despite the abundant resources and general low disease stress experienced by the majority of the population.

The literature on trauma and violence in precolonial North America typically equates it with interpersonal conflict over scarce resources, including resource shortages precipitated by increasing population pressure and unpredictable and fluctuating climate. For example, Walker (1989) demonstrates a pattern of nonlethal blows to the head for groups living on the coast of California and nearby islands. Although there were no significant sex-based differences in the patterning of lesions, men were more frequently involved. Cranial trauma was higher for the Islanders than for the coastal people and he attributes this to intense competition over resources and ritualized violence to diffuse social tensions on the circumscribed island. However, this unidimensional and economic explanation does not fit the data from the American Southwest.

It has been generally assumed that the level of violence perpetrated against women (versus men) is correlated with the relative availability of subsistence resources. For instance, where resources are plentiful (e.g. near permanent water sources in the western deserts), people will "do better," there will be more food to share and to distribute, and there will be less "stress" and presumably less violence; whereas, when resources are scarce there will be an increased amount of "stress" and this will lead to poor health, conflict over scarce resources, and increased violence. However, this is also not the case at La Plata.

A series of hypotheses generated from a political-economic perspective however reveal some interesting alternative possibilities. The La Plata communities were situated in the center of a highly interactive political and economic sphere of influence, and it is likely that an area that provided a stable and abundant amount of resources likely invited an influx of people into the region over time, especially during periods of climate fluctuations in neighboring regions. Consequently, the population living along the La Plata River grew increasingly densely settled, likely due to both in-migration and increased fertility.

A more secure economy may have led to increased population density, decreased mobility, increased political centralization, and perhaps the need for more rigid rules about resource production and distribution. As population density increased, social systems would have to be established to control access to and distribute productive resources, like arable land and food. The communities at La Plata were not likely highly stratified based on available archaeological and bioarchaeological data (see Martin et al., 2010), but there were other social conditions that could lead to status differentiation and inequitable power relations, particularly in control over resources. For instance, some subgroups of individuals likely controlled labor and resource production as well as the differential allocation and distribution of economic resources, creating other underclass subgroups of individuals who did not have the same level of control over or access to those resources.

But why would this underclass at La Plata be primarily young adult women who were routinely battered? Nearly all six women have occipital or lambdoidal cranial modifications consistent with the Puebloan practice of cradle-boarding during infancy, suggesting that they were likely born in neighboring Puebloan communities and not immigrants from distant regions. Domestic abuse in this circumstance is also unlikely to *fully* explain the patterns of injuries inflicted on these women because most adult women from these communities exhibited little to no trauma and were placed in carefully prepared graves with offerings, suggesting domestic abuse of women was not a normalized form of violence in these communities. However, it should be noted here that ethnohistoric and ethnographic research has shown that in societies that practice polygyny or incorporate multiple wives or domestic servants/slaves into the household economies, senior women of the household were frequently perpetrators of abuse toward the subordinate women of the household.

The parsimonious explanation of the differential abuse and indifferent disposal of these six women, therefore, is that they were captive or enslaved women. As will be discussed further in Chapter 4, captive status does not necessarily equate to abuse and mistreatment in all circumstances. Women in Puebloan societies could be both victims and perpetrators of violence (see Chapter 4). While men may have done the initial raiding and capture of women captives, their wives may have been the ones who abused and punished the captive women brought into their households. Furthermore, ethnographic and ethnohistoric research has shown that captive women's experiences of violence in their captor societies were unique to each individual and dependent on the circumstances that fostered their transition into captive status (e.g. retaliation/revenge, adoption), their desirable technological skills and knowledge, and the resources they could use to better their situation and experiences within their captor community. For instance, some captive women may have accommodated their captor's expectations to ensure their survival (e.g. as a co-wife, chore-sister, skilled servant/laborer, teacher) and adapted and assimilated into their new society and social roles within it. Others may have resisted their captors and were abused and/or killed because of their resistance. Additionally, the cranial trauma these individuals sustained, either when they were subdued to be taken captive or while they were incorporated into their captor community/household, also may have contributed to additional experiences of violence and abuse. As discussed above, cranial trauma can also produce significant neurological, physiological, and behavioral changes, many of which may have made it challenging for these individuals to perform the tasks demanded of them within their captor households and communities, and consequently predisposed these individuals to repeated encounters with violence.

Conclusions

The social consequences of intentional violence go well beyond the immediate physical trauma to individuals. Recent research suggests

Figure 3.11 "Patient Toil, Moki Pueblos, Arizona." This image shows a
woman planting seeds while carrying a bundle on her back using
a tumpline. Photo by Detroit Publishing Co. Photo courtesy of
the United States Library of Congress's Prints and Photographs
Division (Digital ID ppmsca.17903). Public Domain. https://
commons.wikimedia.org/w/index.php?curid=11160828.

that "some of the worst and most degrading offenses work by sustaining a palpable threat of violence over a victim without ever having to produce much injury" (Moore et al., 1994: 178). Violence diminishes the daily life of those who are threatened, afraid, or hurt. Studies of violence in contemporary society demonstrate that fear and victimization are not randomly distributed in a population (Warr, 1994: 11). Thus, the study of violence in archaeological contexts must necessarily go beyond the proximate causes of individual cases of traumatic injury. To do so requires the use of a theoretical framework that is responsive to the historical and contextual factors that create and maintain violence.

The memories of violence against women in the La Plata communities have been forever etched into the bones of the women who were beaten and abused. The hard evidence is shown in the healed cranial depression fractures and facial bones, the cases of mobility-related osteoarthritis and asymmetrical joint systems, and the increased amounts of generalized infections. When compared with men and

Figure 3.12 "Young Hopi Indian Woman grinding corn for flour, c. 1900." Photographer: Charles C. Pierce (1861–1946). Photo courtesy of the University of Southern California Libraries and the California Historical Society. Public Domain. https://commons.wikimedia.org/w/index.php?curid=30842348.

women who did not show any head wounds or injuries, these women stand out. Given what is known about the agricultural potential of the area, this was a very good place to live (for some) because there was great potential for rich harvests and year-round food supplies. This is why the area was growing in population during the 1100–1200s. The motivation to carry out raiding on farther away communities in order to capture women and children makes good sense given the need for increasing workers and laborers in the fields and in the homes (Figure 3.11). As this historic photo suggests, being a woman meant a lot of laborious and hard jobs needed to be constantly done, from carrying heavy loads, to planting the fields, to grinding the corn.

Either as captured women from other groups, or as immigrating women from communities that were failing, a group of women were marked as outsiders and their bodies tell a story of abuse and neglect. It is known from historic evidence that Pueblo women spent long hours daily grinding corn (Figures 3.12 and 3.13). The ubiquity of these grinding stations reminds us that hard physical labor was required in

Figure 3.13 "Hopi Indian Woman shelling corn from the cob, ca. 1900." Photographer: Charles C. Pierce (1861–1946). Photo courtesy of the University of Southern California Libraries and the California Historical Society. Public Domain. https://commons. wikimedia.org/w/index.php?curid=30834964.

corn-based agricultural subsistence economies. It is not hard to imagine local women wanting additional help with this laborious task. Captives could fit the bill if they made accommodations to their captive status and carried out the laborious tasks asked of them.

Women's roles have traditionally been homogenized in the literature by both historians and anthropologists in ways that do not permit us to see that all women had multiple identities and played many different roles. The bodies of the women at La Plata reveal the complex ways that violence shaped and impacted their daily lives and, through contextualized analyses, provide us insights into how women in the past negotiated gendered violence both to their benefit and to their peril.

References

Ali, L., & Badar, A. (2021). Management of depressed skull fracture. *Journal of Saidu Medical College, Swat,* 11(1), 30–33. 10.52206/jsmc.2021.11.1.30-33

Bernert, H., & Turski, L. (1996). Traumatic brain damage prevented by the non-N-methyl-D-aspartate antagonist 2,3-dihydroxy-6-nitro-7-sulfamoylbenzo[f] quinoxaline. *Proceedings of the National Academy of Sciences,* 93(11), 5235–5240. 10.1073/pnas.93.11.5235

Bhootra, B.K. (1985). An unusual penetrating head wound by a yard broom and its medicolegal aspects. *Journal of Forensic Sciences,* 30(2), 567–571. https://www.astm.org/jfs11841j.html.

Blackhawk, N. (2009). *Violence over the land: Indians and empires in the early American West.* Harvard University Press.

Brink, O. (2009). When violence strikes the head, neck, and face. *The Journal of Trauma: Injury, infection, and critical care,* 67(1), 147–151. doi: 10.1097/TA.0b013e318182f77f

Brooks, J.F. (2011). *Captives and cousins: Slavery, kinship, and community in the Southwest Borderlands.* University of North Carolina Press.

Cameron, C.M. (2016). *Captives: How stolen people changed the world.* University of Nebraska Press.

Cleveland Clinic (2021). *Osteomyelitis (bone infection): Causes, symptoms & treatment.* https://my.clevelandclinic.org/health/diseases/9495-osteomyelitis.

Colton, H.S. (1960). *Black sand: Prehistory in Northern Arizona.* University of New Mexico Press.

Deloria, V. (1997). *Red earth, white lies: Native Americans and the myth of scientific fact.* Fulcrum Publishing.

Diaz-Arrastia, R., Agostini, M.A., Frol, A.B., Mickey, B., Fleckenstein, J., Bigio, E., & Van Ness, P.C. (2000). Neurophysiologic and neuroradiologic features of intractable epilepsy after traumatic brain injury in adults. *Archives of Neurology,* 57(11), 1611–1616. 10.1001/archneur.57.11.1611

Dobyns, H.F. (1976). *Native American historical demography, a critical bibliography.* Indiana University Press.

Dobyns, H.F. (1983). *Their number become thinned: Native American population dynamics in Eastern North America*. University of Tennessee Press.

Dozier, E.P. (1970). *The Pueblo Indians of North America*. Holt, Rinehart and Winston, Inc.

Dunbar-Ortiz, R. (2014). *An indigenous peoples' history of the United States* (Vol. 3). Beacon Press.

Ember, C.R., & Ember, M. (1997). Violence in the ethnographic record: Results of cross-cultural research on war and aggression. In D.W. Frayer, and D.L. Martin (Eds.), *Troubled times: Violence and warfare in the past* (pp. 1–20). Routledge.

Gannon, M. (2019, September). When did humans reach North America? The question keeps growing more complex. *Discover Magazine*. https://www.discovermagazine.com/planet-earth/when-did-humans-reach-north-america-the-question-keeps-growing-more-complex.

Gonzales, M., & Lamadrid, E.R. (Eds.) (2019). *Nación Genízara: Ethnogenesis, place, and identity in New Mexico*. University of New Mexico Press.

Harris, M., & Ross, E.B. (1987). Population regulation and agricultural modes of production. In M. Harris, and E.B. Ross (Eds.), *Death, sex, and fertility: Population regulation in preindustrial and developing societies* (pp. 37–72). Colombia University Press.

Harrod, R.P., & Stone, P.K. (2018). Mother, laborer, captive, and leader: Reassessing the various roles that females held among the ancestral Pueblo in the American Southwest. In P.K. Stone (Ed.), *Bioarchaeological analyses and bodies* (pp. 191–212). Springer.

Hohlrieder, M., Hinterhoelzl, J., Ulmer, H., Lang, C., Hackl, W., Kampfl, A., Benzer, A., Schmutzhard, E., & Gassner, R. (2003). Traumatic intracranial hemorrhages in facial fracture patients: Review of 2,195 patients. *Intensive Care Medicine, 29*(7), 1095–1100. 10.1007/s00134-003-1804-1

Holsinger, T., Steffens, D.C., Phillips, C., Helms, M.J., Havlik, R.J., Breitner, J.C.S., Guralnik, J.M., & Plassman, B.L. (2002). Head injury in early adulthood and the lifetime risk of depression. *Archives of General Psychiatry, 59*(1), 17–22. 10.1001/archpsyc.59.1.17

Inwood, J., & Bonds, A. (2016). Confronting white supremacy and a militaristic pedagogy in the U.S. settler colonial state. *Annals of the American Association of Geographers, 106*(3), 521–529. 10.1080/24694452.2016.1145510.

Katzen, J.T., Jarrahy, R., Eby, J.B., Mathiasen, R.A., Margulies, D.R., & Shahinian, H.K. (2003). Craniofacial and skull base trauma. *The Journal of Trauma: Injury, Infection, and Critical Care 54*(5), 1026–1034.

Kohler, T., & Turner, K. (2006). Raiding for women in the pre-Hispanic northern Pueblo Southwest? A pilot examination. *Current Anthropology, 47*(6), 1035–1045.

Kranioti, E.F. (2015). Forensic investigation of cranial injuries due to blunt force trauma: Current best practice. *Research and Reports in Forensic Medical Science, 5*, 25–37. 10.2147/RRFMS.S70423

Lambert, P.M. (1997). Patterns of violence in prehistoric hunter-gatherer societies of coastal southern California. In D.L. Martin, and D.L. Frayer (Eds.), *Troubled times: Violence and warfare in the past* (pp: 145–180). Gordon and Breach.

Lee, R.B. (2014). Hunter-gatherers on the best-seller list: Steven pinker and the "Bellicose school's" treatment of forager violence. *Journal of Aggression, Conflict and Peace Research, 6*(4), 216–228. 10.1108/JACPR-04-2014-0116.

Mann, C.C. (2005). *1491: New revelations of the Americas before Columbus.* Alfred a Knopf Incorporated.

Martin, D.L. (2021). Violence and masculinity in small-scale societies. *Current Anthropology, 62*(S23), S169–S181. 10.1086/711689.

Martin, D.L., Akins, N.J., Crenshaw B.J., & Stone P.K. (2008). Inscribed in the body, writen in the bones. In D.L. Nichols and P.L. Crown (Eds.), *Social Violence* (pp. 98–122). University of Arizona Press.

Martin, D.L., & Anderson, C.P. (Eds.) (2014). *Bioarchaeological and forensic perspectives on violence: How violent death is interpreted from skeletal remains.* Cambridge University Press.

Martin, D.L., & Harrod, R.P. (2020). The climate change–witch execution connection: Living with environmental uncertainties on the Colorado Plateau (AD 800–1350). In G.R. Shug (Ed.), *The routledge handbook of the bioarchaeology of climate and environmental change* (pp. 301–315). Routledge.

Martin, D.L., Harrod, R.P., & Fields, M. (2010). Beaten down and worked to the bone: Bioarchaeological investigations of women and violence in the ancient Southwest. *Landscapes of Violence,* 1(1), 3, 1–9. https://scholarworks.umass.edu/lov/vol1/iss1/3.

Milders, M., Fuchs, S., & Crawford, J.R. (2003). Neuropsychological impairments and changes in emotional and social behaviour following severe traumatic brain injury. *Journal of Clinical and Experimental Neuropsychology,* 25(2), 157–172. 10.1076/jcen.25.2.157.13642.

Moore, M.H., Prothrow-Stith, D., Guyer, B., & Spivak, H. (1994). Violence and intentional injuries: Criminal justice and public health perspectives on an urgent national problem. *Understanding and preventing violence,* 4, 167–216. https://www.ojp.gov/ncjrs/virtual-library/abstracts/violence-and-intentional-injuries-criminal-justice-and-public.

Moritz, A.R. (1954). *The pathology of trauma.* Lea & Febiger.

Nolan, S. (2005). Traumatic brain injury: A review. *Critical care nursing quarterly,* 28(2), 188–194.

Ortner, D.J. (2003). Identification of Pathological Conditions in Human Skeletal Remains.

Ortner, J.D., & Putschar, W.G.J. (1985). *Identification of pathological conditions in human skeletal remains.* Smithsonian Institution Press.

Parikh, S., Koch, M., & Narayan, R.K. (2007). Traumatic brain injury. *International anesthesiology clinics,* 45(3), 119–135. DOI: 10.1097/AIA.0b013e318078cfe7

Pringle, H. (2012, November). The first Americans. *Scientific American.* 10.1038/scientificamericanhuman1112-68

Potter, B.A., Baichtal, J.F., Beaudoin, A.B., Fehren-Schmitz, L., Haynes, C.V., Holliday, V.T., Holmes, C.E., Ives, J.W., Kelly, R.L., Llamas, B., Malhi, R.S., Miller, D.S., Reich, D., Reuther, J.D., Schiffels, S., & Surovell, T.A. (2018). Current evidence allows multiple models for the peopling of the Americas. *Science Advances*, 4(8), eaat5473. 10.1126/sciadv.aat5473

Reséndez, A. (2016). *The other slavery:* The *uncovered history of Indian enslavement in America.* Houghton Mifflin Harcourt.

Sarvghad-Moghaddam, H., Karami, G., & Ziejewski, M. (2014). The effects of directionality of blunt impacts on mechanical response of the brain. *Proceedings of the ASME 2014 International Mechanical Engineering Congress and Exposition,* 3: *Biomedical and Biotechnology Engineering.* Montreal, Quebec, Canada. November 14–20, 2014. V003T03A013. ASME. 10.1115/IMECE2014-39338

Spencer, R.F., & Jennings, J.D. (1965). *The native Americans: Prehistory and ethnology.* Harper and Row.

Steeves, P.F.C. (2021) *The Indigenous Paleolithic of the Western Hemisphere.* University Nebraska Press.

Thornton, R. (1990). *The Cherokees: A population history.* University of Nebraska Press.

Titiev, M. (1972). *The Hopi Indians of old Oraibi.* University of Michigan Press.

Trinkaus, E., Churchill, S.E., & Ruff, C.B. (1994). Postcranial robusticity in Homo. II: Humeral bilateral asymmetry and bone plasticity. *American Journal of Physical Anthropology*, 93(1), 1–34. 10.1002/ajpa.1330930102

Walker, P.L. (1989). Cranial injuries as evidence of violence in prehistoric southern California. *American Journal of Physical Anthropology*, 80(3), 313–323. 10.1002/ajpa.1330800305.

Walker, P.L. (2001). A bioarchaeological perspective on the history of violence. *Annual Review of Anthropology*, 30(1), 573–596. 10.1146/annurev.anthro.3 0.1.573

Warr, M. (1994). Public perceptions and reactions to violent offending and victimization. In A.J. Reiss, Jr., and J.A. Roth (Eds.) & National Research Council, *Understanding and preventing violence, Vol. 4. Consequences and control* (pp. 1–66). National Academy Press.

Webb, S. (1995). *Paleopathology of aboriginal Australians.* Cambridge University Press.

Wedel, V.L., & Galloway, A. (2013). *Broken bones: Anthropological analysis of blunt force trauma* (2nd ed.). Charles C. Thomas Publisher.

Wilcox, D.A., & Haas, J. (1994). The scream of the butterfly: Competition and conflict in the prehistoric Southwest. In G.J. Gumerman (Ed.), *Themes in Southwest prehistory* (pp. 211–238). School of American Research.

4   Wives, Mothers, Sisters, Slaves: Complexities in Roles and Relations

Ethnographic/Ethnohistoric Analogies for the Past

Not all facets of Pueblo life, particularly aspects of gendered differentiations and divisions of labor, are visible archaeologically. We turn to ethnographic and ethnohistoric accounts of 16th to early 20th century Pueblo communities for analogies to help us better interpret the patterns we see in the archaeological and bioarchaeological records. These accounts, when critically consulted (see discussion in Chapter 1), provide insights into how individuals within these communities marked gender identities, were socialized into their gender roles, and how, when, and where their respective tasks were performed, which may not be readily apparent in the archaeological record.

Before proceeding, we want to reiterate some important caveats and the importance of critically consulting documentary resources for analogies of past behaviors. First, we must acknowledge that ethnography occurs within the context of unequal and colonial power relations, and the information presented in ethnographic and ethnohistoric sources has been filtered and interpreted through the researchers' own cultural lenses and political agendas (Hatch, 2012: 203). Because of the long history of exploitative contact between Pueblo Peoples and colonial systems, the Pueblos place a very high value on their privacy and are hesitant to allow outside researchers to interview or observe Pueblo members (Jacobs, 1999: 5). Because of this, researchers must exercise prudence when consulting archival sources, autobiographies, and transcribed oral interviews of Pueblo Peoples (Bataille & Sands, 1984: 51–52). While their personal testimonies and biographies shed invaluable light on the experiences, relationships, anxieties, and things Pueblo People considered important in their daily lives (see Nequatewa, 1993; Qoyawayma, 1964; Yava & Courlander, 1978), these individuals' experiences and testimonies tended to be outliers within their communities and not

DOI: 10.4324/9781003123521-4

necessarily representative of the diversity of Pueblo experiences, perspectives, and opinions.

Second, ethnographic and ethnohistoric observations of the Pueblo People were done predominantly by Spanish and Anglo colonial authorities and agents, who projected their own biases and valuations onto the communities they described (Jacobs, 1999: 4). Men and women in Pueblo society held diverse social roles and experiences; however, because of western, Euro-centric biases, many of these sources depict women and men in static, categorically binary ways. European men were socialized to associate working and laboring women with low social status, so when they (rarely) documented women's activities, they tended to misinterpret the labor-intensive activities of the Indigenous women they observed as indicative of the subordination of women to men in Indigenous communities. They also tended to ignore the complementary relationships between genders in the accomplishment of labor tasks (Vivante & Zweig, 1999: 340). Furthermore, ethnographic accounts by European researchers also tended to naturalize and essentialize their perceptions and assumptions about sex and gender relations as fixed and universal within the Indigenous communities they observed, which inhibits us from seeing gender, and gender roles, as fluid social scripts that adapt to the conditions and requirements of the moment (Bruhns & Stothert, 1999: 276).

Finally, we must remember the picture of a culture we get through ethnographies, ethnohistories, and oral interviews is translated and transformed through numerous filters before we, the readers, get it. In reference to his own autobiography, Albert Yava (Hopi-Tewa) observed: "What a person recalls from the past is a combination of what he remembers and what he forgets" (Yava & Courlander, 1978: 1). The person being interviewed speaks to what they know and understand, so the cultural information they provide is filtered through their unique, individual experiences and interpretations of those experiences, and then their testimonies and stories are filtered through the observer/ethnographer's own perception and interpretation of the information being relayed to them (Clifford & Marcus, 1986: 8). Albert Yava also observed that ethnographers and researchers tended to oversimplify the cultural and traditional diversity within and between the Pueblos, which was driven by the constant ebb and flow of people moving among the communities through trade, marriage, and captivity. He also emphasized that it is important for outsiders to understand that no individual or group's culture and practices are universal to the Pueblo People (Yava & Courlander, 1978: 81).

With these caveats in mind, this chapter provides an overview of observations of Puebloan gender roles as described in ethnographic and ethnohistoric accounts, as well as autobiographies and transcribed oral interviews of Pueblo Peoples whenever possible. Elsie Clews Parsons' ethnologies are specifically consulted because her work is notably infused with her interest in the social construction of the individual, particularly the female individual, within the cultural frameworks of the Puebloan communities she observed and interacted with throughout her career. As a prominent feminist anthropologist, Parsons' ethnologies highlight her singular concern with the cultural construction of gender and its lived experience as a social institution (Babcock, 1991: 1), which make them particularly valuable for insights into Puebloan women's experiences of gender (as a social institution) among Puebloan communities in the early 20th century, and consequently as analogies for the past. Furthermore, in the spirit of decolonizing bioarchaeology's approach to studying the past, Parsons is also a noteworthy resource because contrary to the status quo of Anthropology at the time, Parsons insisted that the Puebloan women and men she interviewed, rather than being "invisible informants behind the text [...] appear as authors themselves [...]" whenever possible in her writings (Babcock, 19991: 16).

Ramon A. Gutiérrez's *When Jesus Came, the Corn Mothers Went Away: Marriage, Sexuality, and Power in New Mexico, 1500–1846* is also extensively referenced for its nuanced and holistic discussion of Pueblo lifeways. Gutiérrez's (1991) work is an ethnohistory and ethnology of transculturation, told as much as possible with the words, experiences, and perspectives of indigenous peoples in the American Southwest during the Spanish colonial period. Using Pueblo origin myths and oral histories, early contact documentary sources, archaeological research, and ethnographic and ethnohistoric accounts, Gutiérrez (1991) provides valuable context for the archaeological and bioarchaeological data we observe, giving us an idea of the types of behaviors, practices, structures that produced the boney changes we see and give us a sense of the social meaning behind their patterns and distributions.

In addition to the sources above, we also consult a range of ethnohistories, autobiographies, and transcriptions of oral interviews of Pueblo Peoples, including Albert Yava, a Hopi-Tewa man (Yava & Courlander, 1978), Polingasi Qoyawayma, a Hopi woman (Qoyawayma, 1964), Edmund Nequatewa, a Hopi man (Nequatewa, 1993), and oral stories by the Zuni People (Zuni People, 1972). These accounts demonstrate that Pueblo women held diverse roles, some that conveyed status and social prestige, and others that, in certain contexts, predisposed them to captivity, slavery, abuse, and violence.

Pueblo Social Organization: Status, Power, and Prestige

To understand how social (and gender) roles informed status, power, and lived experiences, we need to understand how Puebloan society operated. Pueblo society broadly revolved around concepts of reciprocity and obligation. To understand how social power, status, and prestige manifested in Puebloan communities and how these relationships impacted people differentially according to sex and gender, a brief summary is offered here, and the authors encourage readers to read Ramon Gutiérrez (1991) for detailed discussions of the intricacies of, and ideologies informing, these practices.

Reciprocity among Pueblo Peoples established an obligatory relationship between the giver and the receiver of gifts of socially desirable goods. Socially desired goods were generally essential items that facilitated the fulfillment of social obligations, ceremonial responsibilities, and social initiations and transitions. These included tangible items like religious fetishes and objects, corn meals and food, ceremonial and/or practical knowledge and skills, religious endowments, and blessings. If a gift is properly reciprocated by a counter-gift from the receiver, then the relationship between the exchanging individuals is equal and no other social debt is owed between the two parties (Gutiérrez, 1991: 8).

Households produced socially desired goods that can be exchanged as gifts to maintain reciprocal social obligations. If you did not have a large enough household to produce the required goods, senior household members or household heads would "indebt" themselves to other highly respected community members who had the desired goods to provide for their households. Indebtedness occurred when you could not reciprocate a gift in an exchange for social goods, so you must pay back the debt owed through labor, respect, and obedience to the individual to whom you are indebted (Gutiérrez, 1991: 9).

Gift exchange was a major component of how transitions between individual life stages, from birth to death, were marked, incorporated, and embodied by individuals and the community. According to Gutiérrez (1991: 8), girls and boys required an accumulation of essential, socially desired goods before they could become adults, or seniors, in Pueblo society. Girls, for example, needed religious fetishes, knowledge about curing, pottery production, how to construct and maintain a house, basket making, and a husband before they could transition from a junior to a senior member of a household. Pueblo boys similarly required fetishes, knowledge of how to hunt, make weapons, and warfare, as well as knowledge in curing, rain-conjuring, and a wife before they could transition to adulthood (Gutiérrez, 1991: 9). However, it was the responsibility of the senior members of the household—parents, grandparents, aunts and maternal uncles, and older married siblings—to provide and secure required goods by offering gifts to other senior members of the community who could provide them (Gutiérrez, 1991: 8).

Consequently, children are indebted to their parents from birth and are expected to reciprocate by being obedient and respectful to their parents and participating in household tasks and production. Girls were expected to help their mothers grind corn, cook, and tan hides, whereas boys were expected to tend to the crops, hunt, and weave. The senior members of the household used the products of the junior members' labor to secure items to be used in gift exchanges with other households so that their children could receive the required blessings and knowledge to get married and become adults, and senior members of society. Failure to adhere to these social obligations was cautioned against in oral traditions and tales, which implied that destruction, chaos, and death would occur to those who do not fulfill the obligations of reciprocity and exchange (Gutiérrez, 1991: 10).

Status and prestige among Puebloan Peoples were achieved by virtue of age, personal characteristics, and skills. As an individual progressed through different physiological stages of life (e.g. infancy, childhood, puberty, adulthood, senescence) and social stages of life (e.g. infancy, childhood, adolescence, marriage, parenthood, elder, etc.), individual power and prestige also grew regardless of biological sex, where both senior adult men and women equally commanded respect and authority within their households and the greater community. In general, senior men were responsible for maintaining the social and religious well-being of the community, whereas senior women were the authorities in everything pertaining to the household, its sacred fetishes, seeds, and food resources (Gutiérrez, 1991: 13). Broadly speaking, the relationships between men and women and their social roles were considered complimentary, mutually interdependent, and balanced among the Puebloans, where men, women, and individuals practicing other gender identities held their own unique forms of wealth, status, prestige and social power within their spheres of action (Gutiérrez, 1991: 13).

Pueblo adults could accrue prestige by possessing desirable knowledge and skills, like hunting, curing, and cultivation, and/or tool and pottery making, and basket or textile weaving (Gutiérrez, 1991: 12). These skilled individuals often received gifts from others who wanted to receive blessings or knowledge from these successful individuals for either themselves or their children. Essentially, among the Ancestral Pueblo during the 16th century, knowledge was power (Gutiérrez, 1991: 26).

Heads of households that had several junior members and/or individuals indebted to them could capitalize on these individuals' reciprocal labor to produce more goods for the household, enabling the household head to support increasingly larger extended households. These extended households could consist of the immediate and extended family, secondary wives, widows, orphans, or stray children, all who reciprocated their social debts through shared labor, obedience, and respect to the head of the household (Gutiérrez, 1991: 12). Therefore, these more "successful" senior members of Puebloan society tended to be the individuals in positions of leadership within the community. These higher-ranking seniors were also the most likely to practice polygyny, acquiring and integrating captives into their households to serve as co-wives, chore sisters, or slaves (Gutiérrez, 1991: 12).

Pueblo Gender Roles and Divisions of Labor

In Puebloan society, the household was the primary economic entity and functioned as a cooperative unit, with every individual member holding a status or position within the social arrangement of the household that was associated with particular responsibilities and tasks which contributed to the household economy as well as the broader community outside of the immediate household. In general, Pueblo boys and men were responsible for activities that required heavy labor, travel outside the village, and securing and supplying raw materials for various household economic production activities. They were responsible for clearing and preparing the agricultural fields with digging sticks and for planting, cultivating, maintaining, and harvesting the agricultural crops (e.g. maize, cotton, etc.), which supply not only the household unit but the community as a whole. Men also are responsible for hunting and fishing for wild game, acquiring and transporting timbers for construction, erecting the timbers for housing and ramada construction, acquiring the clay and making the adobes for house construction, and gathering and transporting firewood for their wife's cooking fires and pottery kilns, as well as acquiring salt and pigments for consumption, crafts, and trade. Men were also responsible for crafts such as weaving, clothing manufacture (e.g. moccasins), engaging in trade that required traveling longer distances from the village, and the manufacture of weapons for hunting and raiding/warfare when warranted (Babcock, 1991; Hill & Lange, 1982; Parsons, 1939).

Pueblo women and girls were responsible for maintaining the immediate household and its economy. Crops were perceived to belong to the women of the household, and consequently they were responsible for

Figure 4.1 "Four Hopi girls grinding corn, circa 1906." Photographer: Edward S. Curtis (1868–1952). Public Domain. Photo courtesy of the United States Library of Congress's Prints and Photographs Division http://hdl.loc.gov/loc.pnp/ppmsca.05085.

processing, grinding, storing, and maintaining the harvested maize from the agricultural fields for consumption and ceremonial purposes (Figure 4.1). Women were responsible for cooking food for the household and ceremonial feasts, fetching water, chopping firewood, gathering wild food resources, cultivating and harvesting the household gardens, as well as weaving baskets and crafting ceramics for personal and ceremonial use as well as exchange. Women were also responsible for spinning cotton, maintaining and facilitating house construction, including plastering the external and internal walls of the house (Figures 4.2–4.4), building their cooking ovens, and facilitating local household exchange in food and commodities (e.g. excess food, baskets, ceramics, clothing, and weavings, etc.) within the immediate village or village cluster (Figure 4.5).

Differentiation between sexes among Puebloan groups appeared in names, speech patterns, kinship terminology, dress, as well as behaviors, practices, and tasks (Babcock, 1991). However, despite the seemingly distinct division of labor between men and women, it was not strictly rigid. In most economic tasks, Pueblo women and men

Figure 4.2 "Two women carrying water from the river to Mishongnovi (Mashongnavi) Pueblo on Second Mesa, Arizona, circa 1898." Photographer: George Wharton James (1858–1923). Public Domain. Credit: University of Southern California Libraries and California Historical Society (http://digitallibrary.usc.edu/cdm/ref/collection/ p15799coll65/id/16855) via Wikimedia Commons https://commons. wikimedia.org/w/index.php?curid=30890922.

engaged in at least a complementary step within the overall processes involved in particular gendered tasks. For instance, women assisted men with the planting and harvesting of the agricultural fields and dressed the meat hunted and butchered by men. Men were responsible for provisioning the firewood and clay for women's cook fires and ceramic manufacture (Parsons, 1939).

Furthermore, gender norms were also fluid among Puebloan groups. If men opted to undertake women's work for an extended period, they were expected to wear women's clothing and conform to women's duties, activities, and behaviors. There was no valuation to this transition among Puebloan groups according to Parsons (1939). She observed that it is permissible, and indeed not entirely unheard of, for a boy or a man (vice versa for a girl or a woman) to culturally change sex where he dresses, speaks, behaves, and performs the duties of a girl or a woman (Parsons, 1939: 104). She also observed that the biologically

Figure 4.3 "A group of Hopi Indian women building an adobe house in the village of Oraibi, ca. 1901." Photographer Charles C. Pierce (1861-1946). Public Domain. Credit: University of Southern California Libraries and California Historical Society (http://digitallibrary.usc.edu/cdm/ref/collection/p15799coll65/id/15586), via Wikimedia Commons, https://commons.wikimedia.org/wiki/File:A_group_of_Hopi_Indian_women_building_an_adobe_house_in_the_village_of_Oraibi,_ca.1901_(CHS-1251).jpg.

male individuals who (in her accounting) had made the cultural change to women made the choice to do so because they either desired or preferred to do women's work and/or because their household was short on women and needed a woman worker for an unspecified period of time (Babcock, 1991: 104). This highlights the fluidity of gender identity and that gender, at least among Puebloan groups, is not exclusively assigned based on biological sex.

Wives, Co-Wives, Sisters, and Daughters

During the 16th and early 20th centuries, marriage marked the transition from adolescence to adulthood, where women generally married around the age of seventeen and men at nineteen (Gutiérrez, 1991: 11).

Figure 4.4 "Hopi woman in the village of Oraibi holding a stone to be used for dwelling construction, circa 1901." Photographer: Charles C. Pierce (1861–1946). Photo courtesy of the University of Southern California Libraries and California Historical Society. Public domain. https://commons.wikimedia.org/w/index.php?curid=30824178.

Marriage was not perceived or practiced as a life-long monogamous institution. Men and women married and, if they desired after a time, could leave and find a new husband or wife. Serial monogamy tended to be the normal practice, however, except for men who accrued enough social power and prestige to acquire additional wives or captives, who they occasionally married and incorporated into their household as co-wives, who were placed under the authority of the first wife (Gutiérrez, 1991: 11).

Figure 4.5 "Moki woman making pottery circa 1900." Public Domain. Credit: Courtesy of Newberry Library, Chicago. Moki Indian Woman Making Pottery, Curt Teich Postcard Archives Collection, via Wikimedia Commons https://commons.wikimedia.org/w/index.php? curid=67016192.

Pueblo communities were matrilineal and matrilocal. Matrilineally organized societies often enhanced women's social status and prestige because ownership of property and particular essential resources lie in the hands of women and are passed down through the female line. Land-use rights, houses, gardens, and household goods were all considered the property of women, who were responsible for distributing it to the household and community (Jacobs, 1999: 7). A typical Puebloan household consisted of the maternal grandmother and her husband, her sisters and their husbands, her daughters and their husbands, young children, possibly a co-wife or slave, and occasionally an orphan or stray child (Gutiérrez, 1991: 15–16). Women tended to stay within their natal household, and men moved between households depending on what stage of life they are in. As children, men live within their mother's household, during adolescence they live in their clan Kiva, and then move into their wife's household once they are married. Even after marriage, men maintain ties to their maternal household and often played a role in the rearing and disciplining of their sister's children (Gutiérrez, 1991: 15–16; Qoyawayma, 1964: 90).

Pueblo houses were built, maintained, and owned by women and were passed down from mother to daughter. The female head of the household was the keeper of the rights and possessions of the household. In addition to owning the house, the female head of the household owned agricultural plots, all the household's food and seed reserves, and curated the sacred fetishes and objects. Women were responsible for feeding the household and would spend hours every day grinding maize and preparing food for daily meals, feasts, and ceremonies, and ritually feeding the household's sacred fetishes and enemy scalps to keep them content (Gutiérrez, 1991: 16).

Within the household, age and sex generally determined what tasks were performed by which members. Typically, junior women and girls were tasked with fetching water, grinding maize, and assisting with food preparation, while more senior women were engaged in repairing and plastering the house, making pottery, weaving baskets, making clothing, and crafting other exchangeable items (Figure 4.5). Junior men and boys tended to the crop fields, hunted, and gathered firewood, while more senior men participated in ceremonials, hunted, wove, and exchanged the goods produced by their household within the community and with communities elsewhere in the greater American Southwest for other desirable items like hides, fetishes, and meat (Gutiérrez, 1991: 17).

Jacobs (1999: 6) suggests that the sexual division of labor within Pueblo communities enhanced women's social status and prestige because men and women held different but equal and complimentary roles. The sexual division of labor did not translate into men dominance and women's subordination (Jacobs, 1999: 6); however, bioarchaeological research has suggested that the strict division of labor tended to result in poorer health outcomes for women, regardless of whether they held higher status within their community, suggesting that their assigned gender roles often predisposed them to higher morbidity and trauma burdens (Jacobs, 1999: 6).

Furthermore, Harrod et al. (2012) found evidence, particularly in societies that practice polygyny (e.g. the Turkana of Kenya), that there tends to be established pecking orders within households with multiple wives, where second wives often worked harder and were beaten more often than the first wife. Harrod et al. (2012) also found that it was common for the first wife to beat the lower status women of the household, including the second wives, drudge wives, or chore sisters, underscoring that men were not the sole perpetrators of violence against women in past societies. While the Pueblos did not extensively practice polygyny like the Turkana, there is ethnohistoric evidence that polygyny was present among the most successful households of Pueblo communities, suggesting that in some circumstances women-on-women violence within polygynous households may have occurred (Gutiérrez, 1991: 12).

Mothers, Grandmothers, and Aunts

In addition to their household responsibilities, women were responsible for the caring, education, and disciplining of children (Figure 4.6) (Babcock, 1991; Parsons, 1939). However, childcare was also an extended family and community-wide responsibility, where the older children and older women helped care for the youngest children and babies while the young women worked grinding maize into meal and preparing food (Jacobs, 1999: 6; Qoyawayma, 1964: 16; Underhill, 1991: 145).

Socialization into gender roles began at birth and progressed in stages as an individual grew, developed, and became able to participate and contribute to the household economy and interact with their broader socio-political world. Generally, mothers, grandmothers, and the other women of the household socialized their daughters, granddaughters, and nieces into their assigned gender roles and taught them how to cultivate and care for the household seeds and food stores, prepare food, make pottery, and weave baskets, and the household prayers, songs and ritual ceremonies that they will be responsible for performing. Men similarly socialized their sons, grandsons, and nephews; teaching them how to make tools, hunt, tend the fields, weave, and perform clan-specific ceremonials and songs (Qoyawayma, 1964: 60).

Older age generally conveyed status and prestige. Consequently, older men tended to labor less in the fields and held ceremonial offices, and taught younger men ritual knowledge and oral histories. Older women similarly labored less in terms of grinding corn and preparing food, which was delegated to the younger women of the household. Older women's responsibilities extended to crafting ceramics and weaving baskets, helping with babies and the younger children, advising and teaching younger women how to make pottery and baskets, and fulfilling the ritual responsibilities of the household (Underhill, 1991: 145).

Figure 4.6 "Hopi Indian mother carrying her baby on her back outside of an adobe dwelling circa 1900." Photographer Charles C. Pierce (1861–1946). Photo courtesy of the University of Southern California Libraries and California Historical Society. Public Domain. https://commons.wikimedia.

Ceremonial Leaders and Keepers of Knowledge

Women's status in social and ceremonial life among Pueblo groups was intimately tied to their economic contributions to the collective work of the household and the broader community (Bruhns & Stothert, 1999: 79). Because of their roles in manufacturing exchangeable and socially desired goods like ceramics, and their technological knowledge of food cultivation and preparation, women's activities and labor products inherently figured into gender relations and status negotiations, placing women in positions of significant importance to household and community economies Bruhns & Stothert, 1999: 93).

Women participated in most ceremonials outside of the immediate household indirectly, typically by preparing and providing food for use in the ceremonies and for the feasting that accompanied them. Initiations into ceremonial societies (sodalities and moieties) marked a change in social status for individuals. For these ceremonials, baskets of corn meal, bread, and meat are prepared and provided by the women of the initiates' families to be shared among the entire community (Ortiz, 1972: 10; Parsons, 1939: 303). Women also held leadership positions and participated in women's ceremonial societies and dances (Jacobs, 1999: 6). Additionally, women were responsible for ritually "feeding" the household fetishes, scalps, and masks to bring blessings to the household (Parsons, 1939: 342). Women as well as men could be shamans and religious leaders, who were responsible for maintaining the well-being of the community and serving as intermediaries between humans and spirits, and acting as healers, diviners, mediators, political leaders, and agents of social control and/or change (Bruhns & Stothert, 1999:169).

While raiding was often perpetuated by men, who would raid crop fields and pueblos for food, resources, and women and children, women also tangentially (and occasionally directly) participated in warfare and raiding activities. Women would send men on raids to procure enemy scalps and women and children captives to supplement household labor. Upon the warriors' return, women would greet the returning war party and take the enemy scalps and "tame" them by stomping on them, chewing on them, and performing derogatory acts on the enemy scalps to remove their malevolent power. Once an enemy scalp had been tamed, it was adopted into the household and become a sacred fetish, where it was the responsibility of the women of the household to ritually feed it and keep it content to convey blessings upon the household (Dozier, 1970: 81; Parsons, 1939: 342). Pueblo women would also similarly assume the responsibility of incorporating captive women and children into their households by teaching and socializing these captive individuals into the specific roles and practices of their communities (Brooks, 1996: 298).

Captives and Slaves

Captives were often young women and children who were taken from their natal communities during raids, becoming commodities enmeshed in a transcultural web of exchange that tied diverse communities together (Brooks, 1996: 280, 2002: 18; Patterson, 1982). They tended to be strangers or enemies to their captor societies, and the context and reasons why they were taken captive likely informed their treatment, with some individuals becoming slaves and others adopted into their captor's household and community (Barr, 2005: 22). Captives who were incorporated into their captor households and societies could become fictive kin through adoption or marriage to their captor (Brooks, 1996: 283). As adopted members of a household, captive women could become clan members, and their children by their captor become members of their father's clan (Brooks, 1996: 287).

Captives were typically taken for labor, sex, procreation, to be abused and killed for revenge, and for the knowledge and technological skills they possessed (Barr, 2005: 23; Brooks, 2002: 287). They were commodities to be acquired or exchanged to increase their captor's social status and to reduce the labor demands on the captor's household or community by providing an additional labor force (Brooks, 2002: 18; Harrod & Martin, 2015: 50). Men were very rarely taken captive, and were usually killed in the fields while defending the community (Nequatewa, 1993: 76).

For example, in Albert Yava's recollection of the events of Awat'ovi massacre, he describes how the chief of Awat'ovi invited warriors from neighboring Pueblos (Wapatki, Oraibi, Mishongovi, etc.) to destroy his village because his people had stopped following Hopi traditions. He asked them to kill all of the men and old women, but to take the young women and children captive to keep their own community populations flourishing, which ultimately preserved some of Awat'ovi's ceremonial societies and associated ritual knowledge and practices within the traditions and practice of these other villages (Yava & Courlander, 1978: 92).

Brooks (2016) presents a transcription of an account by a Walpi woman named Sáliko, who was a descendant of a captive survivor of the Awat'ovi Massacre in the late 1700s (see Brooks, 2016 and Yava & Courlander, 1978 for detailed accounts of the event). Sáliko stated in her account that her ancestor was recognized as the *Maumzrau'mongwi* (Chief of the women's Mamzrau Society) by a man from Walpi who was killing the captive women and children taken from Awat'ovi during the massacre. Sáliko stated that her ancestor was spared execution because she agreed to initiate the women of Walpi into the rites of the Mamzrau Society, and was integrated into the Walpi community as a result. Sáliko also indicated that other women from Awat'ovi who claimed that they "knew how to bring rain" and were willing to teach the songs were spared and taken captive and that a man "who knew how to make the peach grow" was spared and taken captive by men from Oraibi who were also perpetuating the massacre at Awat'ovi (Brooks, 2016: 12). She went on to indicate that it was likely because of this captive man that there was such an abundance of peach trees at Oraibi at the time she provided her account. Similarly, she stated that the men from Mishongnovi who also participated in the massacre at Awat'ovi spared and took captive any woman who claimed to have knowledge of how to make the corn grow or knew song prayers and was willing to teach their captors. Generally, no children were killed during the massacre but distributed as captives among the villages perpetuating the massacre (e.g. Walpi, Oraibi, Mishongovi), however the rest of the Awat'ovi community, except those with specialized knowledge who were taken captive or escaped, were tortured, dismembered, and killed (Brooks, 2016: 12).

While raiding and captive taking was predominantly perpetrated by men, women also played a role in the practice. Wives would encourage their husbands to go raiding for enemy scalps and women and child captives, who would be used to meet the labor demands of the household (Brooks, 1996: 298). Captive women worked under the supervision of the wives of their captors and worked for the household as co-wives, "chore sisters," or slaves (Brooks, 1996: 290). Even if captive individuals were adopted into their captive society, they were likely still treated differently than local women and children and may have suffered abuse at their hands of their captors, captor's wife, or co-wives to coerce the captive individuals into submission and acceptance of their new status (Harrod & Martin, 2015: 50).

Captive women were often multi-lingual because of their captivity, and as a result may have acted as translators, negotiators, and emissaries who facilitated cross-cultural interaction and social ties between groups that were otherwise enemies (Barr, 2005: 21; Brooks, 1996: 286, 2002: 20). Their cultural intermediacy could in some circumstances afford captive individuals a notable amount of agency within their captor societies, and occasionally provide them with an amount of social power and prestige (Brooks, 1996: 286). Additionally, these captive individuals facilitated the exchange of human (genetic), material, ideological, technical, and esoteric knowledge across cultural boundaries; effectively making them agents of cultural exchange and change (Brooks, 2002: 30: Cameron, 2011).

However, even adoption into their captor's household did not always protect a captive from being abused or killed. A transcribed Zuni oral story, "The Return of the Zuni Slave Woman" (Zuni People, 1972), details the experiences of a Zuni woman who was taken captive by the Navajo. While she was gathering water from a spring, a band of Navajo came and took her back to their village. Once there, another captive Zuni woman came to her to interpret what was said between the captive woman and her Navajo captor. According to the other Zuni captive woman, it was forbidden among the Navajo to mistreat captives. The captive Zuni woman was then adopted into her captor's household, where the Navajo women taught her their language and other skills while she labored for them, including the skill of weaving, to help her "be a good wife" (Zuni People, 1972: 43).

The Zuni captive woman lived within her captor society relatively peacefully for several years, until a group of Navajos from another settlement became hostile to her presence and threatened to come to kill her. Her captor decided to marry her to ensure her safety, although the Zuni captive woman was not very pleased with the arrangement because she had come to regard her captor as more of a father figure (Zuni People, 1972: 44). Several more years pass, and she has two sons by her captor husband. The other Navajos again become hostile toward the Zuni captive woman and again threaten to kill her and her children. At this point, to appease the other Navajos, her captor husband decided to leave her, but built her a new house and gave her a share of his sheep to feed their sons. The other Navajos decided that they would come and kill her and her sons in four days, however there was one man among them who did not want to because it was taboo to harm captives (Zuni People, 1972: 44). He warned her and helped her escape the Navajo land, setting her on a course for her natal village in the Zuni lands. When she approached her village, her people nearly killed her because they thought she was a Navajo. However, after she told them the name of her father and that she had been a captive slave who married her Navajo captor, a member of the community remembered that her father had once had a daughter who was taken captive. Once her natal community recognized her, she and her sons were welcomed and integrated back into her father's household (Zuni People, 1972: 51).

Based on this account, we gain insight into experiences some captive individuals may have had. While we do not get the particulars, we can extrapolate that these individuals labored for their captive households, were taught new languages and skills, likely imparted their own skills, knowledge, and technology to their captor's household, and some-times had children by their captors. Their experiences could range from adoption and integration into their captive society where they may have been able to accrue some measure of social power and prestige within their captor society, especially as cultural inter-mediaries because of their multilingualism, or they could become victims of abuse and violence.

Complexities of Women as Captives and Slaves

For most Americans, the notion of slavery likely brings to mind Africans being exploited by plantation owners in the Southern States. Attention has also been paid to the role of the Spanish and slavery in the Americas (Brooks, 2002; Gutiérrez, 1991; Reséndez, 2016). They are often surprised to find out that slavery is not simply a product of colonial expansion but has been around for far longer and is found throughout the world. In general, the most common type of captive taking in the past was where women and children were abducted during an ambush and the men of the community were murdered (Patterson, 1982). This is supported by research that indicates violence against women in the form of raiding and taking captives was a common practice that has been documented in many early pre-state populations (see Cameron, 2008).

The capture of women (and often their children) in raids has been well documented by research from the Northeast and Southwest re-gions of North America. Wilkinson et al. (1997) provide a compre-hensive analysis of nonlethal head wounds from adult males and females from the site of Riviere aux Vase in Michigan (c. AD 1000). What these researchers convincingly demonstrate is that there are clear differences between male and female cranial and facial trauma with three times more injuries found on the women than the men. Additionally, the pattern of these wounds seemed to suggest that they related to efforts to dominate these women and to beat them into submission (Novak, 2006). Ethnohistoric data from historic sources suggest that these early Iroquois-speaking people, who today call themselves the Haudenosaunnee, practiced forms of raiding and cap-ture of women as part of an adaptive strategy to increase the pro-ductivity of individual households.

Similarly, as discussed in this volume, the La Plata sites in New Mexico (c. AD 1000) reveal a high proportion of women with healed cranial and facial wounds. Furthermore, all the women who had been beaten about the head eventually died in their 30s and were buried in abandoned pit structures with no grave offerings. This pattern of being beaten about the head, which causes disorientation, confusion, and submission, is documented by the patterned depression fractures seen on the tops and sides of the women's heads. In a public talk in New Mexico in 1995, Martin et al. presented these findings and suggested that the observed patterns may have been due to domestic violence. Afterward, two elderly Santa Clara Pueblo women came up and offered their opinion. They suggested that we consider that it was the senior women beating the lower-status women who were captured and brought into households to help the wives do their work. Women, not men, were in charge of captive women. While the men may have perpetrated the initial violence during the raids, it was women who were active agents in the continued violence. This led to more research into women-on-women violence in the context of raiding and captivity.

There is a long and complex history of raiding and warfare that was endemic over many generations in past societies. However, the type of violence against women is by no means universal. While the capture and abduction of women and children was likely accomplished through nonlethal domination and beatings in both contexts, the reason for capture and the subsequent treatment of captives was not necessarily similar. In the Riviere aux Vase site, if women captives assimilated and became hard-working members of the Iroquois-speaking groups that held them hostage, they could, over time be adopted and socially accepted into the group. We know this because at the time of death, some of the women with healed head wounds were buried with high-status grave items and other forms of social identification that tied them to the group. Thus, through a process of violence, captive women may have had longer and better lives and even higher status than they might have had prior to being taken captive. In this case, nonlethal violence was used to coerce women into accepting their fate as captives, and once they did so, they were afforded the opportunity to become women with some means.

However, this was clearly not the case for captive women from the La Plata sites in New Mexico. The people living there were the ancestors of the Pueblo Indian groups living in their homelands today. The presence of captive women in this large aggregated agricultural community was most likely motivated by a need for additional labor. All the women with trauma also had several pathologies indicative of habitual hard labor and repeated beatings. This was measured by the number of head and body fractures, the presence of inflammation and wear-and-tear on their arm and leg bones, and the fact that when they did die, they were haphazardly placed in pits without grave offerings (we discuss this in more depth in the following chapters). Women from this site who did not have any of the markers of beatings and hard labor were buried in prepared mortuary pits in a flexed position with many grave offerings. Unlike Riviere aux Vas, these women were not integrated into society, and they were not afforded the same burial treatment as other members of the group. They came into the community as outsiders, were stripped of their identities, but not assimilated into the group, and they stayed that way until they died.

Controlling and capturing women is a well-documented practice in the archaeological past, based on multiple lines of evidence, including patterned trauma on human remains, archaeological reconstruction of mortuary contexts, and ethnohistoric resources. However, the role of captive taking and slavery in the past is only one form of violence perpetrated against women. While rape and sexual assault may also have been part of women's daily lives, these do not leave knowable traces on skeletons, so that aspect has been difficult to measure and demonstrate for past populations.

While many captives likely retained a low or outsider social status within their captor society, making them vulnerable to excessive workloads, disease, and physical trauma, captive or slave status was not always fixed in Pueblo society. Some captives could hold social power and prestige in their own right by possessing desirable knowledge and skills and by being cultural intermediaries and interpreters because of their language skills (Harrod & Martin, 2015: 46).

Captives as Agents of Social Change

Captives were agents of social, technological, ideological, and cultural change. The integration of captive children, adolescents, and young adults into diverse and dispersed social groups throughout the American Southwest naturally facilitated the transmission of ideas, technology, language, social customs, and ideologies with them across cultural and social barriers (Cameron, 2008: 1; 20). Captive individuals would be integrated into their captor or "host" communities via a variety of social practices, including adoption, assimilation, marriage, indentured servitude, or enslavement. The context and nature of their captivity likely informed how captives were integrated into their captor society, as well as their role and treatment within it. Captive individuals could be adopted and integrated fully into their captor society, become wives or concubines, domestic servants or field workers, or slaves (Cameron, 2008: 2).

Captives were taken to increase population, social prestige, and status, and supplement economic production (Barr, 2005: 23; Brooks, 2008: 287; Cameron, 2008: 7; Yava & Courlander, 1978: 92; Zuni People, 1972: 43). Captive taking was a selective process, where old adults and men were killed, reproductive-aged women and children were taken captive (Cameron, 2008: 10). How captive individuals influenced their captive culture depended on how they were integrated and their roles within their captor society (Cameron, 2008: 10–11). Pueblo women may have been taken captive to become drudge wives, under the senior wife of their captor's household (Cameron, 2008: 11). Therefore, captives were active agents of social change, which is likely a reflection of their strategies for survival within their captor societies. They possessed knowledge about agriculture and cultivation, ceramic and basket production, food preparation and techniques, and other technical and esoteric knowledge that could have benefited their captors and their communities, and used that advantage to their benefit (Cameron, 2008: 13).

Summary and Conclusions

Collectively, ethnographic, ethnohistoric, and autobiographical sources and oral histories demonstrate that Pueblo women held numerous diverse and essential positions in their societies. They were property owners; craft, technology, and cultivation specialists; providers of food, clothing, and medicine; wives, co-wives, mothers, and kinswomen; political and religious leaders, medical specialists, and keepers of ritual knowledge; spreaders of culture, language, and technology; peacekeepers, revenge-seekers; and captives and slaves. In this chapter, we demonstrate how Pueblo women's roles and positions in the past were not only diverse but valued and important to the maintenance of their communities. In some circumstances, women's roles were empowering and afforded them a measure of social power and prestige within their respective societies, and in others predisposed them to higher morbidity burdens and risk of being victims of violence and abuse (Vivante & Zweig, 1999: xiv).

References

Babcock, B. (1991). *Pueblo mothers and children: Essays by Elsie Clews Parsons, 1915–1924*. Ancient City Press.

Barr, J. (2005). From captives to slaves: Commodifying Indian women in the borderlands. *The Journal of American History*, 92(1), 19–46.

Bataille, G.M., & Sands, K.M. (1984). *American Indian women: Telling their lives.* University of Nebraska Press.

Brooks, J.F. (1996). "This evil extends especially ... To the feminine sex": Negotiating captivity in the new Mexico borderlands. *Feminist Studies,* 22(2), 279–309. 10.2307/3178414

Brooks, J.F. (2002). *Captives and cousins: Slavery. kinship, and community in the southwest.* University of North Carolina Press.

Brooks, J.F. (2016). *Mesa of sorrows: A history of the Awat'ovi massacre.* W. W. Norton & Company.

Bruhns, K.O., & Stothert, K.E. (1999). *Women in ancient America.* University of Oklahoma Press.

Cameron, C.M. (Ed.) (2008). *Invisible citizens: Captives and their consequences.* University of Utah Press.

Cameron, C.M. (2011). Captives and culture change. *Current Anthropology,* 52(2), 169–209. 10.1086/659102

Clifford, J., & Marcus, G.E. (1986). *Writing culture: The poetics and politics of ethnography: A school of American research advanced seminar.* University of California Press.

Dozier, E.P. (1970). *The Pueblo Indians of North America.* Holt, Rinehart and Winston, Inc.

Gutiérrez, R.A. (1991). *When Jesus came, the corn mothers went away: Marriage, sexuality, and power in New Mexico, 1500–1846.* Stanford University Press.

Harrod, R.P., Lienard, P., & Martin, D.L. (2012). Deciphering Violence in Past Societies: Ethnography and the Interpretation of Archaeological Populations. In D.L. Martin, R.P. Harrod and V.R. Perez (Eds.), *The Bioarchaeology of Violence* (pp. 63–82).

Harrod, R.P., & Martin, D.L. (2015). Bioarchaeological case studies of slavery, captivity, and other forms of exploitation. In L.W. Marshall (Ed.), *The archaeology of slavery: A comparative approach to captivity and coercion* (No. 41) (pp. 41–63). SIU Press.

Hatch, M.A. (2012). Meaning and the bioarchaeology of captivity, sacrifice, and cannibalism: A case study from the Mississippian period at Larson, Illinois. In D.L. Martin, R.P. Harrod, and V.R. Pérez (Eds.), *The bioarchaeology of violence* (pp. 201–225). University Press of Florida

Hill, W.W., & Lange, C.H. (1982). *An ethnography of Santa Clara Pueblo new Mexico.* University of New Mexico Press.

Jacobs, M.D. (1999). *Engendered encounters: Feminism and Pueblo cultures, 1879–1934.* University of Nebraska Press.

Nequatewa, E. (1993). *Born a chief: The nineteenth century Hopi boyhood of Edmund Nequatewa, as told to Alfred F. Whiting.* University of Arizona Press.

Novak, S.A. (2006). Beneath the façade: A skeletal model of domestic violence. In R. Gowland, and C. Knüsel (Eds.), *The social archaeology of human remains* (pp. 238–252). Oxbow Press.

Ortiz, A. (Ed.) (1972). *New perspectives on the Pueblos* (Vol. 10). University of New Mexico Press.

Parsons, E.W.C. (1939). *Pueblo Indian religion* (Vol.1, Vol. 2). University of Nebraska Press.

Patterson, O. (1982). Recent studies on Caribbean slavery and the Atlantic slave trade. *Latin American Research Review*, 17(3), 251–275. https://www. jstor.org/stable/2503176

Qoyawayma, P. (1964). *No turning back: A Hopi Indian woman's struggle to live in two worlds. As told to Vada f. Carlson.* University of New Mexico Press.

Reséndez, A. (2016). The other slavery: *The uncovered story of Indian enslavement in America.* First Mariner Books.

Underhill, R. (1991). *Life in the Pueblos.* Ancient City Press.

Vivante, B., & Zweig, B. (Eds.) (1999). *Women's roles in ancient civilizations: A reference guide.* Greenwood.

Wilkinson, R.C. (1997). Violence against women: Raiding and abduction in prehistoric Michigan. In D.L. Martin, and D.W. Frayer (Eds.),*Troubled times: Violence and warfare in the past* (pp. 21–44). Gordon and Breach.

Yava, A., & Courlander, H. (Ed.) (1978). *Big falling snow: A Tewa-Hopi Indian's life and times and the history and traditions of his people.* University of New Mexico Press.

Zuni People. (1972). *The zunis: Self-portrayals.* University of New Mexico Press.

5 Capturing Women, Capturing Power

The Big Picture

In this case study, we took a close look at how gender violence can be seen as a form of social practice deeply embedded within a myriad of other social practices that are shaped by history, ideology, and cosmology. The aim was to investigate the variable and culturally-specific nature of gender violence while also pointing out the similarities that cross-cut different cultures across time and space. This examination of gender violence is not meant to convey some broad indictment against early Indigenous people. On the contrary, what becomes clear is the ubiquity and antiquity of these practices across time and in different cultures. While some scholars and writers have used the findings of violence in the past to vilify non-White people as well as to romanticize and elevate colonists (Ross, 2021), this study is emphatically not suggesting that all Indigenous people, or even all Ancestral Pueblo people, are violent or inherently focused upon enslavement and gender violence.

What we hope to convey is that violence has a history and a cultural context and studying it in an anthropological and nonreductionist way using more holistic and interdisciplinary approaches clarifies its embeddedness within everyday cultural practices and overarching ideologies. In this particular setting, raiding, the capture of women, and their abuse and forced hard labor were an integral part of a complex approach to "making a go of it" as desert farmers in a marginal and unpredictable environment. Because captivity and slavery are very old practices going back as far as we can go with studying human history, it is important to understand its roots and the ways that it so easily becomes a culturally sanctioned activity. While there were many reasons for taking captives for material gain and to deflect hardship, it was also expedient. For those with political clout or other influential

DOI: 10.4324/9781003123521-5

powers, taking captives solves multiple problems and can be a source of abundant benefit for the perpetrators. The perpetrators, those with power, not only gain wealth in terms of increased resource production, but they demonstrate prowess in raids. The ability of men to add wealth and resources to the general community through raiding for resources and women, whose productive labor they can further exploit, can be a pathway to demonstrating leadership skills and masculinity.

All of this is to say that the violence that is used for cultural practices like captive taking is complex and there are many nuanced and layered meanings for the victims, bystanders, and perpetrators. And, while much of the violence is carried out by men during raids and presumably within households, wives, sisters and mothers may also have engaged in violence against the captives as a show of dominance and to subdue and contain them. It is possible that wives and sisters encouraged the men of the household and community to go on raids when they felt that their workloads were overwhelming and they needed the productive labor that captives brought into the household and community economies. In this case study, it is clear how the violence of captive taking and subordination was normalized within the La Plata River communities because without it these communities would be at risk for starvation and early death of infants and children.

Captives brought new knowledge and traditions into the communities into which they were forced to labor and accommodate. In capturing and commodifying women, communities gained more power in the local and regional arena where important resources were valuable and limited by the vicissitudes of the environment and the climate. More women in households laboring towards production lead to a surplus in food, pottery, and tools, which provided more power from the use of that surplus by men (and some women) to build social and political leverage both locally and regionally.

Captives also bring culture change and cultural diversity in pottery production techniques and design styles, hide production techniques, cultivation, and other forms of material culture (Habicht-Mauche, 2005; Habicht-Mauche et al., 2006). Often women were the keepers of household rituals and oral histories, and who maintained tradition and knowledge of ceremonies and esoteric knowledge important to cultural survival (Cameron, 2016). As discussed in Chapter 4, all the complex roles and identities of women were a factor contributing to the preferential selection of reproductive-aged women in the practice of taking of captives and assimilating them into their various roles within the communities where they lived. Gender violence facilitates this exchange and movement of women and their knowledge from one community to another when other mechanisms for such mobility and transplantation are not possible due to entrenched enmities and breakdowns in communication (Lenski & Cameron, 2018). Additionally, we know from Brooks (2016) that women had specialized knowledge about things like growing peach trees and other valuable crops and were ceremonial leaders of important women's societies, which they used to ensure their survival to be taken captive versus being killed, and to provide their specialized knowledge, techniques, and expertise to their captor community.

The big picture that emerges from all the evidence detailed in this volume implicates socio-cultural (e.g. gender), socioeconomic, and sociopolitical institutions in promoting gender violence and the capture and enslavement of women to consolidate social power and prestige within communities. Political centralization often accompanies increased inequities and the commodification of subordinate classes of people (Cameron, 2016). Coming to these kinds of broader conclusions about the effects of captivity on women and the use of captives to facilitate power relationships can only be achieved if there are multiple lines of evidence taken from multiple sources. This study provides one way to do this by utilizing biocultural and intersectional approaches.

Anthropological Approaches—Biocultural and Intersectional

While scholars often infer the kinds of pain and suffering inflicted on captives, having the bodies (in this case, the skeletons) of these women permitted a much deeper and fuller understanding of the profound effects of gender violence. Their bodies reveal that their individual experiences of disease and trauma was exponentially worse than other members of the community in which they were buried. The suffering and pain they endured while surviving is their circumstances not often the focus of studies on captivity. These women stayed alive, and we see written on their bodies their actions to negotiate their circumstances and their new, forced identities. Interrogating the body politic of captivity framework prompted us to take an even more biocultural and intersectional approach to the interpretation of these individuals' lives. Many variables must be kept in mind when interpreting what life would have been like for these women. The intimate portraits provided through the osteobiographies in this volume demonstrate that there were constraints and challenges to their lives and also agency and resistance by the simple fact that they survived for a period of time as captives and enslaved persons.

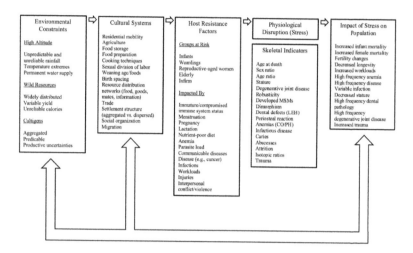

Figure 5.1 The biocultural model of stress.

The model presented in Figure 5.1 provides a shorthand look at all the variables that were discussed in Chapters 2–4. This provides a systematic framework for integrating the information with the larger biocultural and ecological context. In this model, the physical environment is viewed as the source of resources that likely dictated what communities needed to attend to in order to both survive and thrive. If there are constraints on necessary resources, then the ability of the population to thrive may be limited (Figure 5.1, box 1).

Each culture comes up with a unique set of culturally informed activities to meet those challenges, largely through cultural innovations. These strategies and innovations help to buffer the community from things such as starvation and illness (Figure 5.1, box 2). Technology, social organization, and most importantly, the ideology of a group, provide a filter through which environmental challenges and stressors pass. Archaeological work in this region shows that there were a variety of other cultural and behavioral responses likely in operation in the precontact American Southwest to similarly buffer the vicissitudes of the environment and available resources. For example, during periods of low population density, Plog and Powell (1984: 213) suggest that the mating networks of given communities were probably quite large and widespread. As communities became more sedentary and densely populated, social and mating networks would become more proximally located out of necessity. But, if this strategy did not work, capturing women and children and integrating them into the community may have been sanctioned. These two strategies, building alliances and captive taking, may not have been at odds but used in tandem.

As population size and density increased (through a combination of increased fertility and immigration), groups at La Plata may have been forced to organize themselves into cohesive social networks within which food and other resources could be shared (Morris 1939). Alternatively, communities could become increasingly stratified with the inclusion of captives, making some in the community unequal in terms of their access to food and other resources. This would place some members of the group at a higher risk for morbidity and early mortality and could lead to increased strife among competing or oppressed members of the group. All these strategies are complex in their execution and are dependent on a variety of factors.

Although cultural and behavioral responses may have effectively buffered communities during some environmental perturbations, it can be argued that the North American Southwest was marginal enough to produce stressors of a magnitude that could not be effectively buffered. For example, if cultigens were relied on increasingly through time, it would make it difficult to meet dietary requirements should there be crop failure several years in a row. This problem would be compounded if the group size was growing and if there was an investment in a socially rigid set of adaptive strategies to support cultivation and agriculture in a desert environment. In the La Plata case, raiding and captive taking may have helped alleviate stresses on food security. On the other hand, increased sharing, storage capacity, trading, and redistribution of limited resources coupled with flexibility in resource type and procurement could offset the stressors produced by low crop production.

Considering the complex interaction of ecological and cultural/behavioral factors operating overtime at La Plata, ideas about the effects on the body can be hypothesized by consulting a range of medical and clinical literature on disease epidemiology (Buikstra, 2019). Host resistance factors (Figure 5.1, box 3) refer to the fact that not all individuals within a group are equally at risk of increased morbidity and mortality due to stress. Stress originating from ecological and cultural shifts severely affects infants, weaning-aged children, reproductively active women, and individuals with compromised immune systems (e.g. those already ill and/or heavily parasitized and infirm). These individuals are immunologically, metabolically, and nutritionally compromised, especially during times of food resource shortage and high disease loads. Furthermore, conditions like an increase in the risk of experiencing violence and trauma, inadequate diet, and/or physical abuse could disproportionally affect the health of individuals most at risk.

Individuals in good health can often meet the challenge of even a severe stressor. On the other hand, an individual who is suffering from trauma and not in good health may find it difficult to resist even a relatively minor stressor. For example, an infectious disease resulting in gastroenteritis will have a much greater impact on a poorly nourished individual than on one who is well nourished (Noland & Noland, 2020). Because of their biological immaturity, infants are frequently unable to rally from stressors that have only mild effects on a more mature individual. Mortality is particularly high during the first year in many marginal communities (Chavez, 1985). Indeed, Colton (1960:114) states that "the mortality of Hopi children under two years of age is very great, especially after the summer rainy season... very many of the children under the age of two years died of infantile dysentery at Shungopovi".

Adair et al. (1988) present historical and contemporary information on morbidity and mortality in Indigenous groups living in the Four Corners area, within which the La Plata Valley is located. They find that most of the deaths under the age of one were from the pneumonia-diarrhea complex and they observed: "Thus, the most prevalent disease among the living was also the leading cause of death" (1988: 187). Once weaning begins, a second peak in both morbidity and mortality is frequently seen in Third World groups. Infants and young children become dependent on their own natural defenses, at a time when these defenses are just beginning to develop. If nutrition is inadequate, then these defenses will be further hindered. Thus, it is not unusual to see weaning-age infants and children undergoing repeat bouts of chronic diarrhea, upper respiratory disease, and malnutrition.

The inability of an individual to cope with stressors and illness results in physiological disruptions (Figure 5.1, box 4). The severity of the disruption depends on many factors. Age, sex, health status, genetic composition, and nutritional constitution are especially critical factors. For example, a nutritional deficiency that occurs during a critical phase of growth may affect several biological systems. Decreased activity, increased use of fat stores, and decreased skeletal growth are a few of the possible responses. A similar deficiency that occurs after growth ceases may have a little lasting effect on the biological system. Thus, a careful "reading" of subtle morphological changes can be very revealing of physiological disruptions as described in Chapters 2 and 3.

Understanding physiological disruption and the impact of stress on the population feeds directly back into the understanding of cultural buffering and environmental constraints and is presented in the model as a feedback mechanism (Figure 5.1, box 5). It is important to understand the consequences for the community. Poor health can reduce the work capacity of adults without necessarily causing death. Decreased reproductive capacity may occur if maternal morbidity and mortality is high in the youngest adult women (Lettenmaier et al., 1988). Individuals experiencing debilitating or chronic health problems may disrupt the patterning of social interactions and social unity and may strain the system of social support.

In keeping all these intersecting variables in mind, the captive taking of women and children at La Plata can only be appreciated as a complex cultural act. Simplifying it or reducing it to a presumed single cause does not reveal the nuance and cultural specificity involved in captivity for the perpetrators, the victims/captives, and the community members they become indentured into. This model and the use of the three-body theoretical framing consider and integrate many intersecting factors to help us understand the types of violence it engenders.

Working through the Past

Adorno (2021: 157) raises the question: "What does working through the past mean?" While his research focused on explanations regarding the holocaust, he emphatically suggests that working through the past requires attention to complex details and "explication." Explication is different from explanation in that it refers to the process of analyzing and developing an idea in abundant detail. He argues that some scholarly narratives that work through the past tend to silence explication by putting down the "final word" on the event so that it is not further interrogated.

By bringing many different ideas on gender violence, cultural specificity, and the entwined nature of violence and cultural practices at La Plata, we hoped to move along *explication* of the topic more than providing a conclusive and final *explanation*. The difference is important because it invites further interrogation and study. It invites comparing this case of gender violence with more historic and even contemporary cases of gender violence. This approach does not place a priority on the cultural or the biological but rather invites us to further explore where the two meet, in the *biocultural*.

The intimate portraits of these women who were battered and worked to the bone showed that they carried an undue morbidity burden.

Geronimus et al. (2006) have coined the term "weathering" to describe the way multiple stressors—the type caused by discrimination and subordination—leads to premature deterioration of health. In studies conducted by Geronimus (1992) on minority women who face daily discrimination and micro-aggressions, she found weathering to underlie the disproportionately high rates of morbidity, poor health outcomes, and mortality for these women. For the captive women at La Plata, it was the compounding of multiple and repetitive physiological insults. These stressors may have started with nonlethal violence that left them debilitated and cognitively damaged, followed by the increased strain on joints and limbs from repetitive work and increased exposure to infectious disease, and ended with chronic conditions like osteoarthritis, poorly healed injuries, systemic infections, and increased susceptibility to early death.

Epidemiologists and others have long considered this phenomenon as well, and refer to it as allostatic loading (Stewart 2006; Edes & Crews, 2017). Allostatic loading refers to the wear and tear on the body that can accumulate when someone is exposed to repeated or chronic stressors. Given the types and severity of the trauma on the La Plata captive women, it is not difficult to see how repeated injuries and forced hard labor could contribute to the health profiles based on the skeletal changes.

For the mothers, wives, sisters, and slaves living at La Plata, it is important to keep this complexity in the explications that are offered for why there is gender violence. Over 60 years ago, the ethnographers Kluckhohn and Strodtbeck (1961: 298) noted that "Pueblo culture and society are integrated to an unusual degree, all sectors being bound together by a consistent, harmonious set of values, which pervade and homogenize the categories of world view, ritual, art, social organization, economic activity, and social control." In this entangled world-view, it is nearly impossible to isolate any single aspect of Pueblo culture, including violence. Gender violence must be explicated and understood within these broader intersecting realms of people's daily lives. Without doing so, explanations for gender violence in both the past and the present will fall short.

Beating, controlling, and dehumanizing people becomes socially tolerable when it is integrated into the ideology and social organization of communities. Captive women's bodies, visibly wounded, infected, and under constant surveillance, become the canvases on which structural and culturally sanctioned violence acts and is made visible. Theirs is not a simple narrative of victimhood, but it is a story of compromise, resistance, and agency that underscores how gender violence is not one-dimensional, but complex and embedded in relations of power and in the socio-economic, political, and ideological frameworks within which societies operate and sustain themselves.

References

Adair, J., Deuschle, K.W., & Barnett, C.R. (1988). *The people's health: Anthropology and medicine in a Navajo community*. University of New Mexico Press. https://repository.library.georgetown.edu/handle/10822/821376.

Adorno, T.W. (2021). The meaning of working through the past. In V. Pinto (Ed.), *Remembering the Holocaust in Germany, Austria, Italy and Israel*, 157–169. Brill. 10.1163/9789004462236_013

Brooks, J.F. (2016). *Mesa of sorrows: A history of the Awat'ovi massacre*. W. W. Norton & Company.

Buikstra, J. (2019). *Ortner's identification of pathological conditions in human skeletal remains*. Academic Press.

Cameron, C.M. (2016). *Captives: How stolen people changed the world*. University of Nebraska Press.

Chavez, A. (1985). Early life: Nutrition and infant mortality. In F. Falkner (Ed.), *Prevention of Infant Mortality and Morbidity* (pp. 14–27). Karger.

Colton, H.S. (1960). *Black Sand: Prehistory of northern Arizona*. University of New Mexico Press.

Edes, A.N., & Crews, D.E. (2017). Allostatic load and biological anthropology. *American Journal of Physical Anthropology*, 162(S63), 44–70. 10.1002/ajpa.23146

Geronimus, A.T. (1992). The weathering hypothesis and the health of African-American women and infants: Evidence and speculations. *Ethnicity & Disease*, 2(3), 207–221.

Geronimus, A.T., Hicken, M., Keene, D., & Bound, J. (2006). "Weathering" and age patterns of allostatic load scores among blacks and whites in the united states. *American Journal of Public Health*, 96(5), 826–833. 10.2105/AJPH.2004.060749

Habicht-Mauche, J.A. (2005). The shifting role of women and women's labor on the protohistoric Southern High Plains. In L. Frink, and K. Weedman (Eds.), *Gender and hide production* (pp.37–56). Altamira Press.

Habicht-Mauche, J.A., Eckert, S.L., & Huntley, D.L. (2006). *The social life of pots: Glaze wares and cultural dynamics in the Southwest, AD 1250-1680*. University of Arizona Press.

Kluckhohn, F.R., & Strodtbeck, F.L. (1961). *Variations in value orientations*. Greenwood Press.

Lenski, N., & Cameron, C.M. (2018). *What is a slave society? The practice of slavery in global perspective*. Cambridge University Press.

Lettenmaier, C., Liskin, L., Church, C.A., & Harris, J.A. (1988). Mothers' lives matter: Maternal health in the community. *Population Reports*, 50(7), 1–2.

Morris, E.H. (1939). *Archaeological studies in the La Plata district.* Carnegie Institution.

Noland, J., & Noland, D. (2020). Nutritional influences on immunity and infection. In D. Noland, J.A. Drisko, and L. Wagner (Eds.), *Integrative and functional medical nutrition therapy: Principles and practices* (pp. 303–321). Springer International Publishing. 10.1007/978-3-030-30730-1_20

Plog, S., & Powell, S. (1984). Patterns of culture and change: Alternative interpretations. In S. Plog, and S. Powell (Eds.), *Papers on the archaeology of Black Mesa, Arizona*, 1 (pp. 209–216). Southern Illinois University Press.

Ross, L. (2021). Radicalizing montana: The creation of "Bad Indians" continues. In L. Ross (Ed.), *Inventing the savage* (pp. 34–72). University of Texas Press.

Stewart, J.A. (2006). The detrimental effects of allostasis: Allostatic load as a measure of cumulative stress. *Journal of Physiological Anthropology*, 25(1), 133–145. 10.2114/jpa2.25.133

Index